# A NATION IN TROUBLE
## AND MANY DIDN'T CARE

**by William F. Ballhaus, Sr.**

**A.B., M.E., Ph.D., Fellow AIAA,**
**National Academy of Engineering, CE&ME**

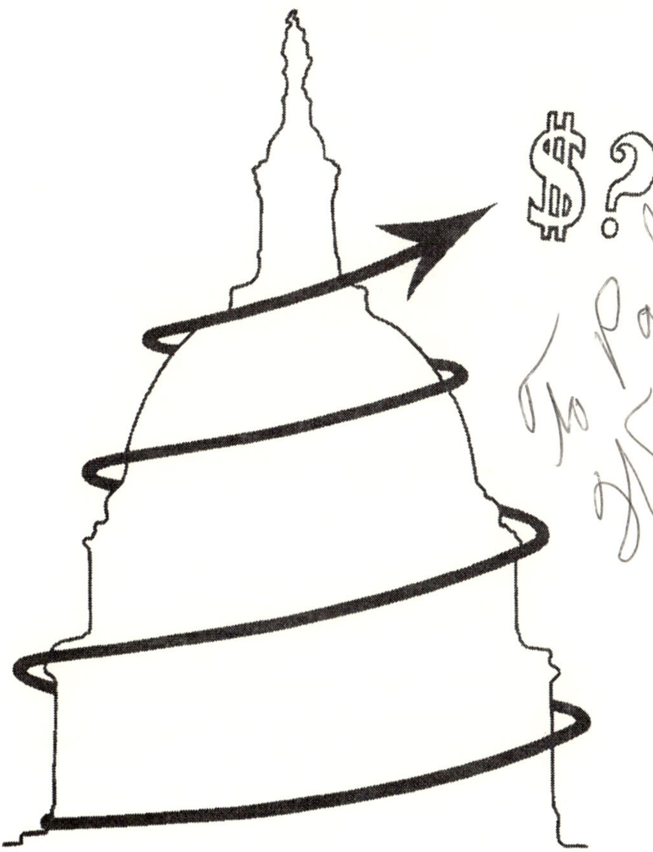


To Paul Sarbanes
Wm F Ballhaus

GATEWAY PRESS, INC.
Baltimore, MD 1996

Ballhaus, William F., 1918-
A nation in trouble and many didn't care / by William F. Ballhaus, Sr.
p. cm.
Includes bibliographical references.
ISBN 0-9653066-0-7
1. Fiscal policy--United States. 2. Budget deficits--United States. 3. Income tax--United States. 4. United States--Economic conditions--1981 - I. Title.
HJ257.2.B35 1996
336.3'0973--dc20 96-28196
CIP

Please direct all correspondence and book orders to:
William F. Ballhaus, Sr.
1293 So. Beverly Glen Blvd.
Suite 408
Los Angeles, CA 90024

Cover and title page art by
Bruce Rydell

Published for the author by
Gateway Press, Inc.
1001 N. Calvert Street
Baltimore, MD 21202

*Printed in the United States of America*

# Table of Contents

# Table of Charts

# Preface

The President, the House of Representatives, and the Senate are locked in a controversy over a so-called "Balanced Budget Program" which they have been misleading the public to believe will result in a truly balanced budget. For the last twenty-six years the United States has not had one year when the budget was balanced—the result has been a Federal Debt growing close to $5 trillion. The so called "Balanced Budget Program" will not produce a balanced budget in any of the next six years—and the result will be a Federal Debt of over $7 trillion. Neither the President, the House, nor the Senate understands what has caused the Federal Debt to rise so horribly.

**Many Didn't Care** is a critical study of the economic history of the United States, reflecting on the history of nations in the past, the early and more modern history of our country, and the vital changes in legislation that have led the country into its current financial difficulties. A condensed history of income tax legislation, starting with the "Beginning" the XVI Amendment to the Constitution, which made it legally possible to collect taxes from individuals, is included to show the path of tax legislation which has led the country to its current critical financial situation.

While many didn't care, some really did care and their positions are contained in this book. Letters from concerned individuals to the Senate Committee on Finance are included and lend credence to the idea that there are many people outside of government that really do care.

Analysis of the economic history reveals economic FACTS not theory, and the facts uncovered are used as a basis for the critical analysis of the effects of tax legislation on the economic performance of our country. It is not whether taxes are high or low, it is whether taxes on savings and investment are high or low. Increased savings and investment should be the motivating factor behind all tax legislation. With a positive climate for savings and investment, our country's severe problems can be solved.

**Many Didn't Care** should provide a broader background and deeper knowledge of the effects of tax policy upon the actions of the nation's people, and should educate the members of the House of Representatives and the Senate as well as the President, and hopefully many of our long suffering taxpayers.

To record how ineffective the Congress has been in reducing Federal Deficits, consider the actions taken and the results achieved. In highly publicized legislation "The Balanced Budget and Emergency Deficit Control Act of 1985" the Congress legislated maximum deficit amounts for the following six years:

For all fiscal years beginning October 1, the maximum deficit amount was ordered:

| | |
|---|---:|
| 1985 | $171,900,000,000 |
| 1986 | $144,000,000,000 |
| 1987 | $108,000,000,000 |
| 1988 | $72,000,000,000 |
| 1989 | $36,000,000,000 |
| 1990 | 0 |

In comparing the actual results with the deficit amounts ordered:

| | | | | |
|---|---|---|---|---|
| 1985 | $212,334,000,000 | — | $40,434,000,000 | over budget |
| 1986 | $221,245,000,000 | — | $77,245,000,000 | over budget |
| 1987 | $149,769,000,000 | — | $41,769,000,000 | over budget |
| 1988 | $155,187,000,000 | — | $83,187,000,000 | over budget |
| 1989 | $152,481,000,000 | — | $116,481,000,000 | over budget |
| 1990 | $221,384,000,000 | — | $221,384,000,000 | over budget |

The Congress passes laws that it completely ignores. Observing the economic performance of the country after passing this so-called "Emergency Deficit Control Act," it is clear that the Congress truly does not understand what steps must be taken to really gain control of our country's revenues and expenditures. In 1985 the Congress obviously knew the country was in economic trouble, and passed what was supposed to be an emergency bill. It is apparent that their tax and spend programs were not even close to balancing, and they still do not realize that the sure way to increase tax revenues to meet ever-expanding spending programs is to improve the rate of savings and investment by our citizens so that the nation will grow economically at a rate much greater than our rate of population growth. Significant reductions in the taxes on savings and investment are essential to changing the course of our economic performance.

There is no other way!

Even though the Congress failed to live within the limitations established by the "Balanced Budget and Emergency Deficit Control Act of 1985," they tried it again: On September 29, 1987 Public Law 100–119 the "Balanced Budget and Emergency Deficit Control Act of 1987" restricted maximum deficits amounts to 144 billion, 136 billion, 100 billion, 64 billion and 28 billion dollars in each of the following five years starting in October 1, 1987.

Again the Congress could not live within the fiscal boundaries established by Public Law 100–119, as indicated by the following results: Deficits in each of the following years amounted to:

| | | | | | |
|---|---|---|---|---|---|
| October 1, 1987 | — | $149,769,000,000 | — | $5,769,000,000 | over |
| October 1, 1988 | — | $155,187,000,000 | — | $19,187,000,000 | over |
| October 1, 1989 | — | $152,481,000,000 | — | $52,481,000,000 | over |
| October 1, 1990 | — | $221,384,000,000 | — | $157,384,000,000 | over |
| October 1, 1991 | — | $269,521,000,000 | — | $241,521,000,000 | over |

No significant improvement in the personal, private investment climate was initiated by the Congress, so there was no way that the nation could even come close to reaching the stated deficit restrictions. It is absolutely essential that the Congress pass legislation that will substantially improve the personal, private investment climate to drive real economic growth to levels experienced in years prior to the enactment of the Tax Reform Act of 1969. Real economic growth as high as 4.5 to 5 per cent per year will automatically generate tax revenues at levels sufficient not only to balance Federal budgets, but will eventually create surpluses, so that payments can be made to reduce the currently horrible debt now exceeding $5 trillion.

The present controversy between Congress and the Administration is really a fight about cutting spending, which is necessary, but there does not appear to be any radical change in tax policy which will significantly improve the personal, private investment climate that is essential to any improvement in the financial performance of our country. Again, significant reductions in taxes on savings and investment Will motivate our people to save and invest, and drive the nation's economic engine. There is no other way.

# Introduction

> The budget should be balanced, the Treasury should be refilled, public debt should be reduced, the arrogance of officialdom should be tempered and controlled, and the assistance to foreign lands should be curtailed lest Rome become bankrupt.
>
> —Cicero 63 BC

While Cicero may not have had the publishing technology of our day, his many letters and orations demonstrated his vast knowledge of the affairs of governments and men. His wit, fire, humor and breadth permitted him to handle complex problems with a perfection of style and form such that none of his critics, ancient or modern, question his supremacy in Roman oratory, and history.

His vision in recognizing the apparent problems of irresponsible Government spending and financial management, and almost unconscious regard or understanding of the problem of an ever increasing Government debt, should serve to awaken all people to the problem of a Congress and Administrations that seem to believe that debt does not matter. Debt does matter and it is necessary that our Congress and our President understand that it does.

Our country's problems of continuing Federal Deficits and ever-increasing Federal Debt can be solved. Over the past 26 years your author has heard from all quarters, as a trustee of a college, as a councilor of the National Academy of Engineering, as a member of the Board of Visitors of a Medical School almost all laments have been, **"We must cut, cut, cut!"**

These words, **"Cut, cut, cut"** disturbed your author. In such a country having so much resource, so many fine people, and most important our valued Constitution, **cut** was abhorrent. The answer should be grow, grow, grow economically, then the resource and wealth created by that growth would permit the country to pay its bills and provide all the services needed by its citizens. That same economic growth would provide the financial resources—federal revenues—not only to balance the budget, but to create surpluses so that the horrendous Federal Debt can be reduced in a long term program to solve that problem. The old adage, "In time of Peace prepare for war" can be extrapolated to "In time of Peace pay your debts." Even our new fledgling country in the early 1800's paid down significant amounts of debt that was necessary to finance the Revolutionary War and the War of 1812. Even after World War I the country generated substantial surpluses that made it possible to reduce the debts that had piled up during the War. The last year of surplus was 1969, and since that time deficits have followed deficits so that in late 1995 the President was requesting a raise in the debt ceiling to nearly $5 trillion, an incomprehensible amount to the average person.

# Prologue

My original intent in creating this book was to point out some of the problems facing our country, and hopefully, to propose some solutions to many of our country's serious problems. As I studied more and more of the history, not only of our country, but of other civilizations as well, it became clear that this book had a much deeper meaning and purpose.

History Prior to 5,000 BC did not seem to be relevant, but the governmental systems of Ancient Egypt did lend some support and understanding to the notion that governments could create some policies to improve the quality of life of its citizens. The fall of Egypt from its advanced position in art and architecture, as well as its sound-financial accounting system, did not seem to be important to providing insight into the problems facing our nation today, but it was interesting to find outstanding positive policies to improve the PRODUCTIVITY of the country, even in those days.

A study of the Economic history of Europe became much more relevant, and was important to concluding that investment is absolutely necessary to the economic growth of any nation. That important fact seems to be completely forgotten in the halls of Congress and in our administrations. They talk about economic growth but they don't know how to motivate people to make it happen, and to make it happen on a continuing basis.

When I first started to write, I felt that a detailed history of the Income Tax would be the basis of the book. To me it seemed that the Beginning was the XVI Amendment to the Constitution, the amendment that gave the Federal Government the power to levy taxes directly on its citizens and other residents. While that history alone is interesting to contemplate, and must be central to the problems of our nation, it alone is not sufficient to provide the background of knowledge needed to arrive at solutions to our country's serious problems.

The economic history of Great Britain and the history of our Country prior to 1913 provide powerful messages to us all and lend credibility to the positions taken in the book. History can be a great teacher, and economic history can lead to knowledge and understanding which might provide background to arrive at solutions to the serious economic problems of our country.

In arriving at the title "Many Didn't Care," it was modified from "They Didn't Care," because some did care and did try to change things to help the country, while others really didn't care; and there were others who either were ignorant or insidious and really didn't care, or tried to carry their own agenda, and to hell with the country and its problems!

Please don't think of the discussions in this book as economic theory: they are economic facts, facts that can lead to solutions to our country's pervading and serious problems, problems which can be solved if we act in time!

Read on and learn what can be done to have our country resume its position as the world's leading power economically, militarily, diplomatically, and socially. We can be the best country in the world to raise children, and to provide a good life for its citizens.

The author's experience as an aerodynamicist taught him to look for information in the data presented to him by wind-tunnel tests, to find the story behind the data. He learned to use the data to design aeroplanes and missiles. What is important is that the obscure story told by the data had to be interpreted and corrected to arrive at useful information which was critical to the design of aircraft that had never before been designed. As the author studied economic data he was impressed by the incorrect interpretation by many economists of the data available to them.

The original intent of this book was to study the history of our income tax laws and to try to derive from that study the effects of changes in those laws over the years. One section of the book does cover the history of the income tax laws over the years since 1913, which is considered the BEGINNING. The author thought it would be much more revealing to understand some of the history of other countries and their economic performance. There are brief references to the economic history of Europe, which references led to powerful support to the author's contention that investment is essential to the economic growth of a country.

The author found that there is a 25-year prohibition in the Senate and a 30-year prohibition in the House of Representatives on releasing information sent to the Senate or the House by the country's citizens. Nevertheless, the author has included some letters from concerned citizens sent to the Senate to try to improve the country's tax laws. One letter accused the Federal Government of fraud, others attacked the current tax policies, and still others complained about spending policies. It is felt that such letters are representative of many of the concerns of private citizens who went far enough to write to the Senate Finance Committee at that time.

While the author felt that almost no one cared about the terrible financial performance of our country, he wanted to include some opinions and beliefs of other citizens who did care. And there is a complete section referring to articles written, positions taken, and suggestions made by many well-known Senators and Representatives and even one Governor.

Finally, discussion of our present financial predicament, and the tax policies that got us to that point, analysis of the profound effect of savings and investment on the economic performance of our country, and the suggested changes in our tax laws that will motivate our country's citizens to save and invest to create: the jobs needed by our ever-growing population, new technologies, new products, improved productivity, more tax revenues to balance our out-of-balance budgets, and annual surpluses so that we may start to reduce our horrendous Federal Debt.

The book demands action by our people, our Senators, our Representatives, and our President to get this country moving again to resume its economic as well as military and diplomatic positions of leadership. It is not too late.

CHAPTER ONE

# A Nation's Serious Problem

## *They Didn't Care*

No one seemed to sense that our country was threatened by a serious slide from a position of world leadership in economic, diplomatic, and military power. Such a threat was not posed by external forces, for no people or country had the power to threaten our position of leadership. The threat came from our own House of Representative, our own Senate, and yes even our own President.

No one seemed to understand or recognize the retrogressing but continual changes that had taken place to cause our cascading fall from the richest, most productive country in the world to a struggling, deficit ridden, and debt ridden nation barely able to compete in the world marketplace. There is still hope for a return to our leadership position, but we must study and understand the events that led us down a path of high unemployment, continuing Federal Deficits, and an ever-increasing Federal Debt. The Federal Debt alone must be confronted and considered a serious threat and menace to the future of our country. Our Federal Debt today is of such an incomprehensible magnitude that it could cause the ruination of the United States as we know it. Over the centuries prior civilizations and nations have been ruined by their leaders' inattention to the severe problems of fiscal irresponsibility and short-sighted policies.

As Santayana has said, **"Those who cannot remember the past are condemned to repeat it."** We must learn from history!

It will not help to study Pithecanthus Erectus and his development 300,000 year ago. Neither will it help to study Neanderthal Man of 100,000 years ago. Pry as we may into the habits and customs of Cro-Magnon Man 35,000 years ago, our prying will not give us a clue to finding our way out of our nation's present serious predicament.

Historians are not certain about and still argue about the date when the Egyptians first brought forth their calendar of 12 months of thirty days with five festival days at the end of each year. Whether it was 5650 BC, or 4241 BC, or 2781 BC will not help us to solve today's critical national problems.

It is agreed that the Egyptians created a most remarkable highly centralized and efficient fiscal system for collecting taxes. Their system was far superior to the methods and procedures later used by the Romans. The objective of the Egyptian government was to make the country economically strong and productive. Certainly our government leaders should be adhering to that objective.

In ancient Egypt the assessment and collection of taxes were carefully monitored by central authorities. Current balance sheets and records of receipts and expenditures were reported to the Pharaoh each month. All of this was carried out 2,000 years before Christ! The Egyptians had developed outstanding arts and crafts, and excellent architectural capabilities even though they did not have iron or steel they were able to erect the pyramids, obelisks, and other enduring monuments. The lesson to be learned from Egypt is that their government objective was "to make the country economically strong and productive."

In the pages that follow we will study more modern history and the important lessons that can be learned to understand what has caused the fall of the United States from its pre-eminent position in the world. More importantly, we will show the critical changes that must be made to reverse the downward trend and restore the economic power that is essential to the leadership of the United States.

## *Federal Spending of Nations*

In the last ten years the Federal spending of the United States has averaged 22 per cent of Gross National Product. In the ten years after 1954 spending averaged only 18.3 per cent of GNP. In those same ten years Federal Deficits averaged only 0.59 per cent per year.

While a change in average spending from 18.3 to 22 per cent doesn't seem very substantial, at the 18.3 per cent level the United States had a balanced budget in 2 out of the ten years. At the 22 per cent level there has never been a balanced budget, and the Federal Debt has soared to $5 trillion! And budget deficits have hovered around 5 per cent of GNP—ten times that level experienced in the ten years after 1954.

The most frugal national government in 1994 was Germany at a level of total government spending of only 2.9 per cent of their Gross Domestic Product. Germany's tax policy motivates their people to save more than twice as much as U.S. people, and further motivates investments at a level nearly 50 per cent higher than the investment level in the U.S.

France was the second most frugal national government in 1994, total government spending was at 5.6 per cent of GDP.

Great Britain was next in line with 6.3 per cent of GDP in 1994, followed by Spain at a level of 7.0 per cent of GDP.

Italy spent at a level of 9.6 per cent of GDP in 1994.

How is it that these countries can provide all of the services for their people at levels of less than one-half that of the United States? And for Germany the people are fully served at one-tenth the level of the U.S.?

Could it be that the real economic growth over the last 26 years in the United States has not been sufficient to provide services to its ever growing population? That certainly is the answer.

Prior to the Tax Reform Act of 1969, for nine years real economic growth averaged 4.335 per cent per year. Since 1969 real economic growth has ranged from 1.6 to 2.2 per cent per year.

In a study of the total tax revenues collected over the last 50 years, the level of tax revenues averaged near 20 per cent of GNP. If the real economic growth of the U.S. had remained at the 4.335 per cent level over the last 26 years, in 1995 the Federal budget would have enjoyed an $850 billion surplus. The power of compound economic growth over the years would have helped the country solve its serious financial problems of continuing Federal Deficits and incomprehensible Federal Debt.

Although Federal spending is considered to be out of control by some people, it could be that our problem is that we have not had sufficient real economic growth over the last 26 years. We can do something about increasing the rate of real economic growth. Our House and Senate could enact legislation which would improve the investment climate for individuals, to motivate them to invest heavily in the future of the country. The tax law of 1954 is one law which motivated substantial investments, but we need more improvement in the investment climate than was provided in that law.

## *The Critical Decision to Invest*

The decision to invest does not necessarily come easy. It takes courage to invest, to take the risk of failure with the prospect of eventual gain. But the decision is critical, since when one decides to invest one has also made the decision to defer consumption—investment by one definition is simply deferred consumption. That critical decision has two profound effects: Investment increases supply of goods—and the deferred consumption decreases demand for goods. Those two phenomena working together eventually drive prices down.

Further benefits of the decision to invest creates new jobs, permits the development of new technology, increases economic growth, improves international competitiveness, and eventually provides more taxes to finance our Federal government. A fifty year study of the total revenues collected by the Federal government indicated that such revenues remain relatively constant as a percentage of real gross national product. In other words if more Federal revenues are required the Government should establish policies that would foster much higher real economic growth.

The critical decision made every pay day by individuals either to invest or to consume is much more important than one would assume. A study was made of four companies having sales volume of 0.5, 1.0, 2.0, and 20 billion dollars. Each of these companies creates annual tax revenues from at least six sources: Corporate income tax; corporate social security tax; corporate unemployment tax; employee social security tax; employee income tax; corporate shareholders tax on dividends received.

For every dollar of sales on the average the total taxes paid to the Government amount to about 10 or 11 cents. Thus for every dollar used to buy these companies' products, a consumer contributes 10 or 11 cents to Federal revenues. If instead of purchasing the company's products, an individual invests in the company's equity, and stays invested for as long as 10 years, during those ten years the revenues would approach 30 or 33 cents per year and the present value of that stream of tax revenues would approach 3 dollars, since each year the revenues would grow as the companies grew. One can see that the purchase of a dollar's worth of product occurs only once, but the ten-year equity investment continues to work and grow.

This very simplified analysis shows how important the fostering of investment is to the future financial strength of the country. Every dollar invested rather than spent on consumption inures to the benefit of the Federal Government, by a very large factor.

Even a communistic country like China has learned that investment is essential to the total well-being and standard of living of their people. They are going in the right direction and we seem to be going in the wrong direction with respect to motivating people to invest in the future of their country.

## *Shareholders of Public Corporations*

In 1978 the New York Stock Exchange published data concerning the number of shareholders of public corporations as a per cent of the United States population.

After the passage of the 1954 Internal Revenue Code, the level reached about 5 per cent of the population in 1955. In the next 15 years there was a continual growth in shareholders up to over 15 per cent. The rate of growth per year was at a level of 7.49 per cent.

After the passage of the Tax Reform Act of 1969, there was a significant reduction in the percentage of shareholders to about 9 per cent by 1978. That loss of shareholders was at a rate of 5.5 per cent per year. That's a decline of 13 per cent per year.

In the fifteen years from 1955 to 1970 the population grew 42.5 per cent. A simple computation shows that the number of shareholders grew at the rate of over 10 per cent per year, from 1955 to 1970. It is clear that the 1954 Internal Revenue Code motivated individuals to invest in the future of their country. The motivation was provided by the significant difference between the tax rate on gains from investment and the ordinary income of individuals. The long term capital gains tax rate was a maximum of 25 per cent and the ordinary income tax rate was as high as 91 per cent. At the highest levels there was a most important pressure on individuals. The pressure could be defined as the "Pressure to Invest."

The pressure to invest can be computed as the after tax return on long term capital gains divided by the after tax return on ordinary income, and at the highest levels of income is:

$$\text{PRESSURE TO INVEST} = \frac{.75}{.09} = 8.33$$

The concept of the pressure to invest is most important in driving the populace to invest more rather than to earn more.

Individuals are not stupid or ignorant, by 1969 30.8 million individuals had invested in public corporations. When the pressure to invest was lowered by the 1969 Tax Reform Act to 1.15, investors fled investment in public corporations and by 1975 reached a level of only 25.27 million.

That reduction in the number of investors brought with it a reduction in the investment in equities of $103 billion. That loss in capital brought with it the loss of over 4 million jobs and unemployment rose from 2.8 million in 1969 to 7.4 million by 1976. A further effect of the loss in equity capital drove interest rates from around 5 per cent in 1969 to as high as 16 per cent, as companies had to enter the debt markets to acquire the capital they needed to invest in new products, new technology, and productivity improving new equipment.

These results of the horrible changes in the investment climate caused by the ill-conceived 1969 Tax Reform Act are not empty economic theory but the realities of the reactions of individuals to truly bad tax policy. The lack of investment also caused the real economic growth rate to decline from a level of over 4 per cent per year to less than 2 per cent per year, and has resulted in year after year Federal Deficits contributing to our current incomprehensible $5 trillion Federal Debt. That history certainly should provide enough lessons to be learned, and lead to proper, sound tax policies in the future.

## *The Importance of Investment to Productivity*

One of the most enlightening studies made by the author during his campaign to change the tax laws of the United States was the study of investment ratios of three countries: Japan, Germany, and United States. Average investment ratios for these three countries over a period of thirteen years were computed based on the data in the "Capital Goods Review" published by the Machinery and Allied Products Institute in 1976. The report showed total investment ratios as a per cent of gross domestic product for the years 1960 to 1973.

The average investment ratios for the United States, Germany, and Japan over those thirteen years were 13.9, 19.1, and 26.9 per cent, respectively.

Another important study was the productivity increases for the three countries over the same period. Productivity increases were taken from the "International Economic Report" of the President to the Congress in 1976. The average productivity increases of the United States, Germany, and Japan over the thirteen years from 1960 to 1973 were 3.29, 5.85, and 10.05 per cent per year, respectively. When the investment data and the productivity data were combined and related to each other there was a striking conclusion: Productivity is directly dependent on Investment. In other words, if a country wishes to improve its overall productivity, it must encourage investment. (Chart I on the following page.)

When the author studied the nine years prior to 1969, United States performance showed an average productivity increase of 3.23 per cent per year. For the six years after 1969 the average productivity increase dropped to 1.529 per cent averaged over the six years to 1975. Productivity increases fell 52.7 per cent after 1969.

Loss in productivity was only one of the significant arguments developed by the author to convince the Congress and the Senate that the tax laws should be changed.

Another argument developed was the study of Annual Growth of the Real Gross National Product prior to 1969 and subsequent to 1969. The President's International Economic Report to the Congress of 1977 showed a growth rate of 4.335 per cent per year averaged over the nine years from 1960 to 1969. For the six years after 1969, the growth rate averaged only 1.657 per cent per year—a drop of 71.8 per cent.

The precipitous drop in rate of growth of the Gross National Product as a result of the decrease in investment motivated by the Tax Reform Act of 1969 was a further argument used to convince the House and the Senate to change the tax laws.

Additional studies showed that tax revenues collected are directly related to growth in GNP, and the reduced rate of GNP growth eventually caused Federal Deficits as high as $73.7 billion by 1976.

This information further substantiated the author's proposals to change the tax laws to motivate individuals to invest in the future of their country. Evidently the arguments were understood and the tax changes were made in 1978 and 1980. Over those years the

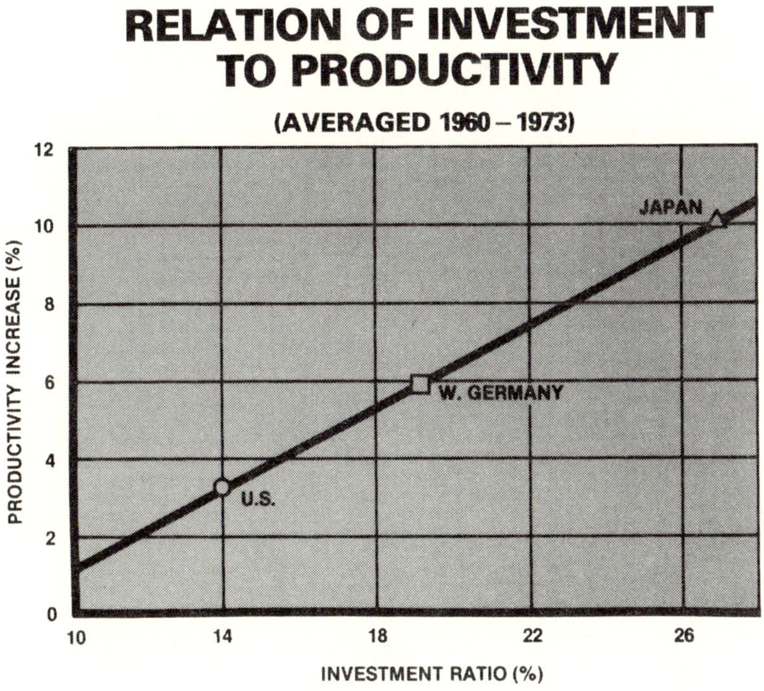
RELATION OF INVESTMENT TO PRODUCTIVITY
(AVERAGED 1960 – 1973)
PRODUCTIVITY INCREASE (%)
0
2
4
6
8
10
12
10
14
18
22
26
INVESTMENT RATIO (%)
U.S.
W. GERMANY
JAPAN

Chart I

capital gains tax rates were lowered from 49.125 to an eventual 20 per cent, maximum. Individuals responded to the changes by increasing their investments. The overall economic performance of the country started to improve, but eventually that improvement was negated by the 1986 Tax Changes. Uncertainty became the most unsettling part of the tax law—uncertainty caused by complexities of the minimum tax and the higher taxes on capital gains.

## *A Scholarly Approach*

Ms. Mai Nguyen Woo created her doctoral dissertation, "A Time-Series Analysis of the 'Lock-in' Effect of Capital Gains Taxation in the United States,"[1] in partial fulfillment of requirements for her Ph.D. degree in economics from Georgetown University in Washington, D.C. The important conclusion Woo reached was that a tax rate between 10.5 and 11.5 per cent would maximize the total revenue received from taxing long term capital gains.

Woo pointed out that under present law, a capital gains tax is imposed on the appreciation of capital assets only when the assets are sold or otherwise disposed of. Because this is so, the owners of capital assets may hold them longer than would otherwise be the case, as a means of avoiding the gains tax. This is known as the "lock-in" effect.

Several studies have found that high tax rates significantly deter individual investors from realizing capital gains. Analysts have therefore concluded that a reduction of gains tax rates would induce substantial unlocking through realization of deferred gains, and thus increase tax receipts. Revenues, however, will not continue to increase indefinitely as gains tax rates are reduced. It is therefore important to ask, "How far can the capital gains tax rates be cut without a downturn in revenues?"

If we encourage more realizations by reducing the rate of tax on capital gains, as we did in 1978, two things occur. First, the reduced rates increase the level of realized capital gains. Second, the increased realizations have the longer-run effect of depleting the stock of accrued capital gains. In other words, the realization of additional gains as a result of cuts in capital gains tax rates reduces the size of the pool of accrued gains—which in turn determines the level of gains realizations in future years.

There has been much discussion about the required holding period for gains to be considered as "long term." Shortening the required holding period for capital assets merely shifts what would otherwise be taxed as short-term gains into the long-term category. Since long-term gains are currently taxed at 40 per cent of the rates applicable to short-term gains, it follows that the revenue effect of shortening the required holding period will be negative, and that tax receipts will decline at least in the short run.

Woo indicates that there are several existing econometric studies finding that the tax elasticity of capital gains realization is greater than unity; e.g., a 10 per cent reduction in the gains tax rates would induce investors to realize more than 10 per cent additional long-term capital gains. Some analysts, therefore, have concluded that lowering the capital gains tax rates would increase revenues via substantial "unlocking." But this is only a short-term effect. A new econometric model which estimates the permanent effect of changes in the tax rates on capital gains realization over time, is now available. Such a study concludes that the short-term effect of cuts in capital gains tax rates is positive, from a tax revenue standpoint. Longer-term effects reduce the stock of potential gains, which is a crucial determinant of the amount of realized gains in future years.

What is not treated in the dissertation is the effect of reducing the long term capital gains tax rates on the individual's specific decisions to invest rather than to consume—that is the critical personal individual decision to invest in the future of the country. Those decisions to invest by millions of taxpayers truly make the difference between a strong growing powerful economy and a debt ridden deficit plagued economy. Those millions of taxpayers deciding to invest in the future of their country provide the capital to create new products, to develop new technologies, to improve productivity, to increase real economic growth, to provide new jobs for a growing population, an to improve our negative international trade balance.

Most econometric studies fail to take into account the vast changes that occur when there is a change in the after-tax total return on personal private investment. The critical criterion is AFTER-TAX RETURN!

The lessons of history are very clear. Let's look at what happened after the Tax Reform Act of 1969 was passed by the Congress and signed into law by Richard M. Nixon.

For the nine years prior to 1969 the consumer price index rose at a compound growth rate of only 1.78 per cent. After the passage of that law, the consumer price index grew at a much higher rate and reached a level of 12.2 per cent in 1974.

While the labor force grew 14.7 per cent from 1969 to 1975 the number of investors shrank 18.1 per cent from 30.8 million to only 25.27 million. That's a loss of 5.53 million investors. Since the labor force had grown from 80.7 million in 1969 to 93 million by 1975, if the same percentage of the labor force had continued to invest there would have been 35.5 million investors so the loss is really more like 10.23 million people who were no longer interested in investing in the future of their country. (Chart II)

At the average level of investment by individuals in 1975 of $10,100 that amounted to a loss of almost $103 billion of investment capital that was no longer available to corporate America.

Companies raising new equity capital numbered 1800 in 1969, but by 1975 only 150 companies raised new equity capital. What is even more alarming companies of 5 million net worth and smaller raised 1.103 billion in new equity capital in 1969 yet by 1975 only 16 million was raised in new equity capital. The number of small companies—raising equity through public issues of securities decayed from 649 in 1969 to only 9 of such companies going to the market. According to Department of Commerce reports of 1974, small companies created new jobs at a rate 66 times greater than large mature companies, because of their own faster growth rates. (Charts III and IV on following pages).

Unemployment of 2.8 million grew to over 7 million in the years from 1969 to 1975. By 1975 over 4 million new jobs were needed to reduce the unemployment rate to 3.5 per cent—a level that is considered an irreducible minimum rate.

# LABOR FORCE UP SHAREOWNERS DOWN

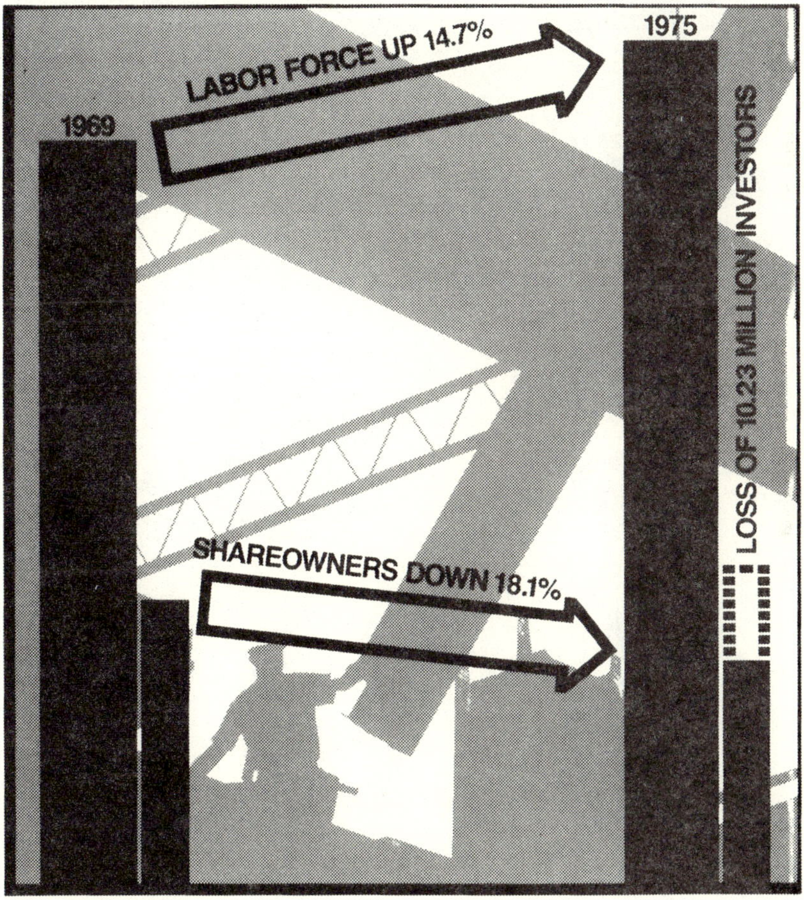


**Chart II**

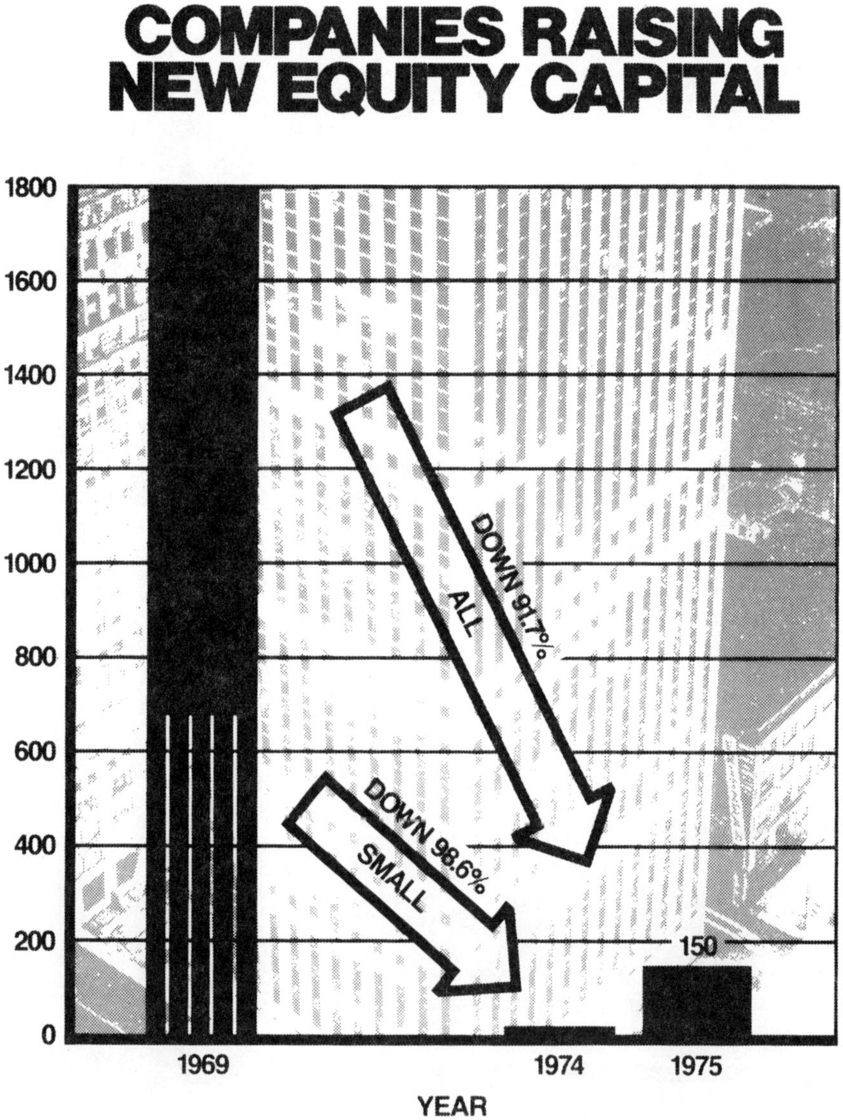
COMPANIES RAISING NEW EQUITY CAPITAL
1800
1600
1400
1200
1000
800
600
400
200
0
DOWN 91.7%
ALL
DOWN 98.6%
SMALL
150
1969
1974
1975
YEAR

Chart III

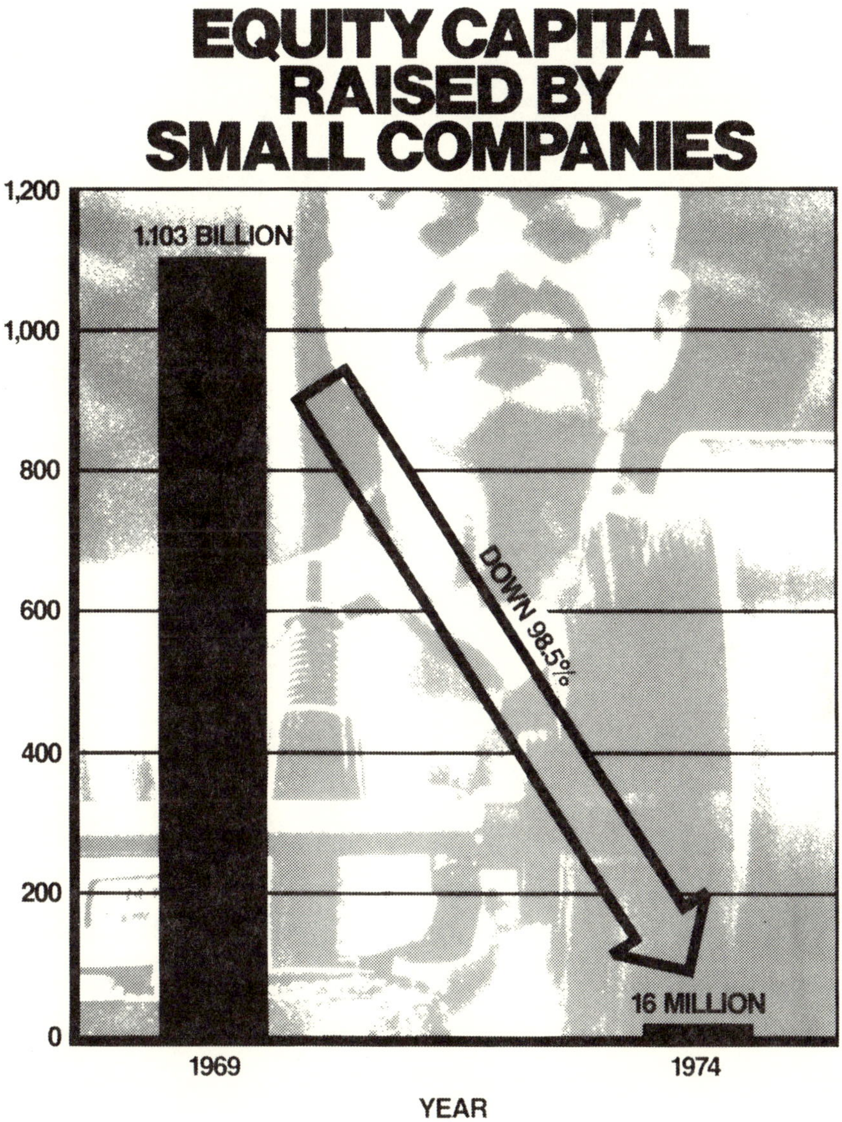
EQUITY CAPITAL
RAISED BY
SMALL COMPANIES
1,200
1,000
800
600
400
200
0
1.103 BILLION
DOWN 98.5%
16 MILLION
1969
1974
YEAR

Chart IV

What is even more devastating to the economy, small technical companies floated new public issues at a rate of 200 per year in 1969, yet by 1975 only two small technical companies floated new equity issues to raise much needed capital to create new jobs, new products, and advanced technology. What an economic tragedy.

History has shown that tax policy has a tremendous effect on the economic performance of any country. The results of the 1969 Tax Reform Act certainly gives proof that tax policy can cause the total deterioration in the performance of a national economy. The decline of the merchandise trade balance is shown in the Chart V.

## GROWTH AND DECLINE— U.S. MERCHANDISE TRADE BALANCE

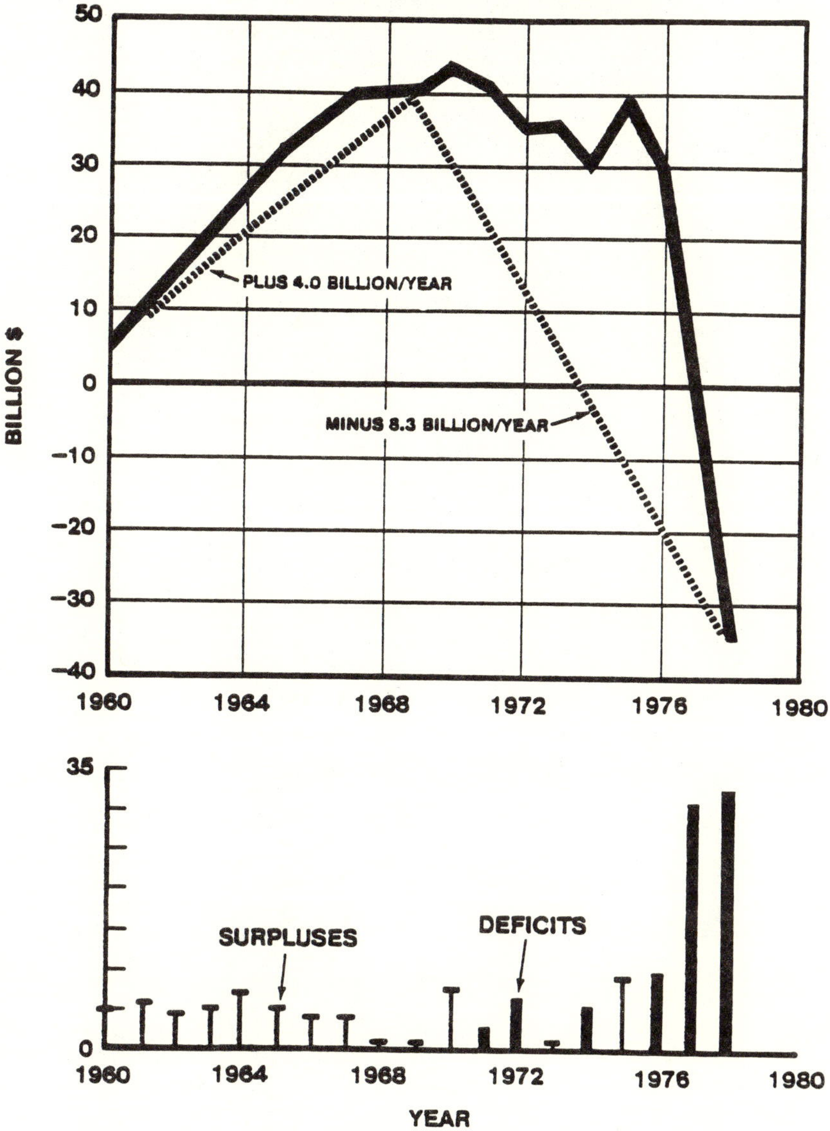


Chart V

## *The Arithmetic of Capital Gains Taxes*

There are two aspects of the arithmetic of capital gains taxes. One aspect is the after-tax return of any capital gain; the other is the "lock-in effect."

The after-tax return is easy to calculate. If the maximum tax rate is 49.125 per cent, the after-tax return is the pre-tax return times 50.875 per cent. At that high tax rate the required return for any new investment to be made, after liquidating the original investment, would be at most over 95 per cent higher than the original investment. When the investor is confronted with such a high rate of return to be required on any new investment, the investor is reluctant to liquidate the original investment. That "reluctance" is the "lock-in effect." The lock-in effect severely limits the mobility of capital, that is, the freedom to move capital from one investment to another investment. This reduced mobility of capital is not good for the economy because it restricts the ability to invest in the most attractive investment and therefore is detrimental to the effectiveness or the efficiency in the use of the available capital stock. Thus the country's economy suffers.

Further important aspects of the arithmetic of capital gains are the return to investors at various capital gains tax rates, and maximizing the tax revenues provided by various capital gains tax rates.

In the 1920's the tax rate for capital gains was 12.5 per cent. The after-tax rate of return was the pre-tax return times 87.5 per cent. After the passage of the 1976 Tax Act the maximum rate for capital gains was 49.125 per cent, and the after-tax return was as calculated above.

In the 1920's the required re-investment return was only 14.3 per cent higher than the original investment return. After 1976 the required re-investment return was 7 times higher than that for the 1920's investor, or 96.5 per cent.

Not only was the original investment decision much easier in the 1920's, but it also was much easier to make an investment change. The higher tax rate in 1976 not only made it much more difficult to make the original decision to invest, but it also was much more difficult to make an investment change.

It is simple to conclude why investment dropped after the 1969 and 1976 tax acts. The 1969 act raised capital gains rates to a maximum of 42.5 per cent, and the 1976 act went further and raised the maximum rate to 49.125 per cent. The risk-to-reward ratio increased significantly under both tax acts. Productivity dropped, real economic growth declined, unemployment soared, and inflation reached a high approaching 13 per cent, with interest rates approaching 15 or 16 per cent, and with trade balances falling from positive to negative with our international trading partners.

There is no question that tax policy was largely to blame for the United States decline as an economic power, with continuing Federal Deficits, and a soaring Federal Debt.

## *Another Effort to Improve the Economy*

In February of 1982 the author convinced the leading Republican member of the House of Representatives Committee on Ways and Means to introduce a bill to the 2nd Session of the 97th Congress. That bill was H.R. 5587 and was a bill "To amend the Internal Revenue Code of 1954 to provide for the non-recognition of gain on the sales and exchanges of capital assets when the proceeds are re-invested in securities issued by domestic corporations."

Section 1041 of that bill provided that so long as an investor re-invested the total proceeds of any sale or exchange of any capital asset within a year of the time of sale or exchange, there would be no recognition of the gain for tax purposes. The basis of the property or asset so sold or exchanged would remain as the original basis of the asset sold or exchanged.

Such a bill really treats the sale or exchange of capital assets as a "roll-over" and there is no tax consequence of any sale or exchange. What is important here is that all capital assets are free of the "lock-in" problem which occurs under present tax law. Such freedom to change and choose new investments is terribly important to the freedom of capital—so that capital can move to the most advantageous investments at any time. Such a provision is important to the total investment climate—since there are no impediments to the best and most proper investment at any time. An investor can move his investments from say the steel industry to the microbiology industry which may be more advantageous to the country at the time without serious tax consequences. That is a most important freedom of investment.

"Rollover" has been recognized in the sale and purchase of a personal residence, and in the treatment of mergers and acquisitions in all tax legislation over the years. The roll-over provision is essential to the total freedom of capital investment.

Treasury studies have determined that such a provision would reduce total tax revenues, but their analysis is done on a static basis, and so does not take into account the dynamic effects of the freeing up of all capital in the country. Such dynamic effects are the maximizing of the benefits of freedom to invest, the dynamics of the freedom to invest in the most productive investments at any time, and the unlocking of static investments to free up capital to be invested in the most profitable and most productive areas.

Such studies also do not consider the effect of motivating individuals to make that critical decision to invest rather than to consume. Such a provision would certainly motivate individuals to invest because of the freedom not only to make the first investment, but also to change an investment when the investor so desires. That freedom is terribly important in improving the investment climate for individuals.

H. R. 5587 was not passed because the Treasury did a static analysis and reported to the Congress that there would be a revenue loss from such a provision. Such a static analysis is total hogwash, almost no studies by the Treasury Department consider the dynamics of the economy—the effects of motivating individuals to change their patterns of activity. The powerful effects of tax policy upon the investment climate are never considered. Often Treasury studies show that a cut in tax rates will lose tax revenues for the Treasury, and increases in tax rates will gain revenues. Many times the reverse is actually true. For instance, when the capital gains tax rate was cut in 1978 and 1980, instead of losses in capital gains tax revenues in the years following the cut in tax rates, capital gains tax revenues increased.

When capital gains tax rates were increased in 1969, revenues from capital gains declined considerably. The dynamics were simple to understand: when higher tax rates are high enough, individuals don't take any capital gains—when rates are reduced individuals can afford to pay the reduced taxes, so they make the choice to take the gains and pay the reduced taxes. These two lessons of history are clear, yet our policy-makers haven't seemed to learn the significant effects of tax policy upon the activities of individuals.

It is seen over and over again, that tax policy should encourage individuals to save and invest, and tax policies should include a series of provisions that would insure that individuals are not passively investing, but rather, are actively saving and investing to their own benefit—and consequently, to the benefit of the nation.

CHAPTER TWO

# Exposing Economic History Pertinent to the Solution of Our Country's Serious Problems

Originally, the author thought that the story should start with the "BEGINNING," that is the start of the income tax law created by the XVI Amendment to the Constitution ratified in 1913. Extensive research by the author led him to believe that more background and history would lend credibility to the proposals for legislation to solve our nation's serious problems of continuing Federal Deficits and ever-increasing Federal Debt.

Brief studies of ancient history proved to be unimportant to arriving at solutions to our country's problems, although some concepts of governments in antiquity were useful in determining that the government could create an atmosphere to motivate people to be productive.

Economic studies of England between 1760 and 1860 brought to light important conclusions that investment was increasingly necessary to provide real economic growth.

The first acts of the Congress of the United States established agencies of the Federal government, and provided for financing the operations of the government. Those acts also provided for payment to Congressmen and Senators as well as the Justices of the Supreme Court and the President and the Vice President.

The first Secretary of the Treasury, Alexander Hamilton, was to set the tone for the financial operations of the new nation. Although Hamilton made many enemies because of his strict adherence to fundamental and sound financing practices, his motivation was to build credit-worthiness and integrity in the new government, and he succeeded.

The Revolutionary War had taken its toll in the significant growth of Federal Debt—but that was necessary to bring a successful conclusion to the campaign. After the war debt was reduced.

The Louisiana Purchase also required the new government to raise an additional $15 million to finance that increase in land and resources. Subsequent to the purchase, debt was continually reduced.

The War of 1812 was financed by further borrowing, but after the war the government continued to reduce its outstanding debt.

One of the heroes of that war eventually became President, and established a goal of paying off all Federal Debt. Andrew Jackson had been an unschooled attorney, a former Congressman, an erstwhile Senator, a territorial governor, a major general of the regular army, a rough and tough prosecutor and a businessman. Jackson was defeated in the election of 1824; although he received the most electoral votes for the Presidency, the House of representatives awarded the Presidency to John Quincy Adams. Jackson eventually won the next election in a smashing victory over Adams in the election of 1828. Many attributed his victory as a repudiation of the policies of centralized government in Washington and the tendency to interpret the Constitution too broadly. He eventually reached his goal of zero Federal Debt, an unheard-of accomplishment by any administration.

During depressions and wars debt was always increased, but after such difficult times the government reverted to a program of reducing debt. It is interesting to study in more detail the actual financial accomplishments of this fast-growing nation.

## *Acts of the First Congress of the United States*

The first Congress of the United States created the War Department, the Department of Foreign Affairs (Department of State), Treasury Department, and other agencies of the Country. From a tax standpoint, Statute I Chapter II "An act for laying a duty on Goods, Wares, and Merchandise imported into the United States" was to provide some source of revenue while Chapter III "An act imposing duties on tonnage": 6¢ per ton on US owned ships, 30¢ per ton on foreign owned ships built in the US, 50¢ per ton on all other ships to be paid annually.

Of course, the members of the House and Senate had to enact legislation to provide for their own pay, and that was Chapter XVII "an act for allowing compensation to the members of the House of Representatives and the Senate of the United States, and to the officers of both Houses" Compensation consisted of $6.00 per day, for each day the member sits in his house plus $6.00 for each 20 miles for travel from his residence to his seat in Congress, prior to March 4, 1795. After March 4, 1795 allowance for Senators was raised to $7.00. Chapter XVIII provided for compensation to the Chief Justice of the Supreme Court at $4,000 per annum and each Justice would receive $3,000 per annum.

Chapter XIX provided compensation to the President of $25,000 per annum paid quarterly, and $5,000 to the Vice President.

The first Congress was faced with constructing an entire Government with all of the required agencies, and when you think of the work that lay ahead for these legislators, it truly was a monumental task.

The intent of the Congress was to establish a total government that would carry out its responsibilities of protecting the people in their peaceful pursuits by its War Department, and carry out its international responsibilities with its Department of Foreign Affairs, in addition it created the Treasury Department to hold its funds and to insure that the financial responsibilities of the nation were met and carried out in a timely manner. The first Secretary of the Treasury, Alexander Hamilton, may have created a host of enemies by insisting that the country not only borrow money to meet its current obligations but that it properly pay interest when due, and repay all loans when due, so that this new nation would build a reputation as a country that could be trusted, a nation of the highest integrity.

All credit should be given to the first Congress for a job well done. To establish an entire government from top to bottom in the period of less than a year, and to provide for the financing of that government's operations by providing a revenue stream from very specific taxes levied upon ships and products of all kinds is a commendable achievement. Providing a system of expending the nations funds through its various agencies was also a herculean task.

Much credit should be given to Alexander Hamilton, and it might be interesting to consider some of his concepts and observations. Hamilton was the student of many contemporary governmental conceptualists and he based many of his actions and admonitions on the philosophies of some of these advanced thinkers of his day.

## *Alexander Hamilton's Views*

Hamilton suggested that a **"Motive to greater exertion in any occupation could be created by raising taxes—not so high as to discourage industry by engendering despair, but high enough so that everyone would have to work in order to pay them."** Hamilton believed that government could bring about changes in the economy which in turn would alter society for its own benefit. He was also committed to private enterprise and to a market economy. And the function of government should be to promote a general spirit of improvement. It should reward productivity and punish dissipation, idleness, and extravagance. Taxes should be designed to encourage industry, never to impede it.

Detailed observation of the activities of the Treasury Department following the Revolutionary war showed that the federal Government had a commitment to reduce the Federal Debt in a continuing program:

> By the first of January of 1801, the Federal Debt stood at $81,996,268.49 and in the next two years the debt was reduced to $78,750,669.83 and $74,728,023.98. The Louisiana Purchase caused the Government to raise further debt to handle that transaction so that it reached $85,349,744.35 by January 1, 1804. In the following three years the debt was reduced to $80,530,159.78, $74,539,058.75, and 67,727,756.76, respectively.

This is a remarkable performance by a fledgling new nation fighting to build its credibility and its credit-worthiness in a doubting world. Such a performance was a result of the steadfastness of Alexander Hamilton, the then Secretary of the Treasury, in meeting the demands of creditors throughout the world. His unbounded integrity as manifested by his performance in building the financial strength of the new nation overcame most of the criticism of his strong fiscal policies. He believed that integrity was essential to the future of the new nation.

If we contrast his performance to the present performance of our House and Senate since 1969, you find that fiscal responsibility is nowhere to be found in the halls of the Congress or in the offices of the Administration. The last year of a Federal surplus was in 1969, a year when the United States had a positive Merchandise Trade Balance of $40 billion. Since that year the U.S. has had ever growing Federal Deficits and declining trade balances, until today the Federal Debt is over $5 trillion and the trade balances are negative and approaching $100 billion. What a horrible performance!

Hamilton's belief that taxes should be a motive to a greater exertion in any occupation, but not cause despair, yet cause everyone to work to be able to pay them, is fundamental to a positive tax policy. His further belief that government could bring about changes in the economy to alter society for its own benefit, is still true today —but what we need is a government that understands the powerful force of motivation of its citizens to act in a manner beneficial to the whole of society. Motivating people to invest in the future of their country could be the most powerful action that the Congress and the Administrations could take to get our country growing again to provide products for its ever-growing population, to provide jobs for the growing work force, and to create the economic growth necessary to provide sufficient tax revenue to balance the Federal Budget and eventually to make payments to reduce the horrendous Federal Debt. Hamilton was correct in his belief that taxes should encourage industry, not impede it. He was also correct in believing that government should reward productivity and punish dissipation, idleness, and extravagance. Certainly productivity is one of our most pressing problems in the battle for the world's markets. We could use a man like Hamilton in today's House and Senate and in the White House!

## *Some Ideas and Concepts of Government*

In the 17th century John Locke proposed some arguments of the nature of governments, "In some distant past, man had existed in a state of nature, wherein he had been endowed by God with inalienable rights to life, liberty, and property. Because men are imperfect creatures, however, some violated the rights of others. For their mutual defense, men banded together and formed governments, whose sole function was the protection of individuals in their natural rights. As long as a government rested upon consent and performed its function, it was legitimate and must be obeyed; if it ceased to do so, those living under it had the right to abolish it and erect a new government that was more likely to do its proper job. The doctrine justified civil disobedience whenever, in the judgment of people affected by particular laws, government trespassed upon the natural rights of any body of citizens or subjects."

Basing his ideas on the above concepts of government, even Alexander Hamilton, one of the early patriots who really cared for his country, wrote, "When the first principles of civil society are violated, and the rights of a whole people are invaded, the common forms of municipal law (meaning legislative enactments and judicial decisions) are not to be regarded. Men may then betake themselves to the law of nature." Hamilton really did not believe in mob action but had an interesting reaction to the Boston Tea Party, "A small number of people provoked by an open and dangerous attack upon their liberties. All they did was destroy a parcel of tea that was merely the private property of a gigantic and monopolistic corporation, The East India Company."

One of Hamilton's mentors was David Hume who conceded, **"Honor is a great check on mankind.** But, where a considerable body of men act together, this check is in a great measure removed." This principle is so potent that the whole body **"acts as if it contained not one member who had any regard to public interest and liberty."**

Perhaps these principles are indicative of what is wrong with actions taken by men of honor who as members of the House of Representatives and the Senate continue to take irresponsible actions, actions that appear to be completely oblivious to the severe problems of continuing Federal Deficits and soaring Federal Debt. Certainly the House and the Senate contain a considerable body of men acting together. Over the years the House and the Senate have passed numerous laws, and as Locke observed, "Where there is no law there is no freedom." Hamilton believed that what the nation needed was, "Individuals of established reputation and conspicuous for probity, abilities and fortune." And Hume believed, "Of all men that distinguish themselves by memorable achievements, the first place of honor seems due to legislators and founders of states, who transmit a system of laws and institutions to secure the peace, happiness and liberty of future generations."

Your author has been trying to do good for the country ever since his campaign to change the tax laws in 1977, which changes he was able to convince the House and the Senate to enact. But something must be amiss—because Jacques Necker 18th century French Minister of Finance said, **"Youth is the only time for an ardent desire of doing good: it is perhaps the only season, in which we believe in virtue, or at least are charmed by the magic of it."** Even at my age, I still believe I can make changes for the good of our country —that's the reason for taking the time to write this book.

## *The Early Financial History of the United States*

Total receipts into the Treasury from March 4, 1789 to December 31, 1791 amounted to $10,210,025.75 and during that time period a total of $7,207,539.02 was expended out of the Treasury to pay for all Government services, and to repay some public debt of $5.238 million. As of December 31, 1791 receipts from customs amounted to $4,399,473.09, and miscellaneous income was $19,440.10. The rest of the receipts were from loans and treasury notes of $5,791,112.55.

The financial operations of the new nation were in good order as a result of Alexander Hamilton's persistence in building a record of paying creditors in a timely manner and convincing lenders to lend to this new nation which was carefully gaining a reputation of integrity and financial responsibility.

The War of 1812 caused the country to borrow extensively over the 1812 to 1815 Period. The first year $12,837,900.00 was borrowed, and $26,184,435.00, $23,377,911.79, and $35,264,320.78 was borrowed in 1813, 1814, and 1815, respectively. These borrowings were necessitated for expenditures ranging from $22,279,121.15 in 1812 to a high of $39,582,493.35 in 1815.

The Revolutionary War caused commodity prices to rise significantly during the war, but after the war prices subsided to pre-war levels. The same price experience occurred during the War of 1812, and again after the war prices fell to pre-war levels.

Over a period of 25.5 years from March 4, 1789 to December 31, 1815 total Federal Expenditures amounted to $378,447,443.69. Revenues for the same period amounted to $391,553,136.57. That performance left a total differential of $13,105,692.88, at the end of 1815. This represented a most commendable performance for this new and growing nation. Government spending rose from $13.6 million in 1811 to $22.3 million in 1812 and topped out at $39.2 million in 1813. Such spending receded to $38,028,230.32 in 1814, but rose again in 1815 to $39,582,493.35. A total debt provision of $12,628,922.35 at the end of 1815 enabled the new growing nation to start a program of debt reduction over the ensuing years.

Revolutionary War expenditures made it necessary to borrow from foreign sources, and by 1801 the total amount of foreign debt stood at $10,419,000. Government management was such that each year foreign debt was reduced: foreign debt was reduced by $504,000; $1,185,000; $2,994,000; $1,671,000; and $1,836,000 in 1802 through 1807, respectively, so that foreign debt was reduced to only $1,420,000 at the end of 1807. Such financial performance by the new nation was truly appreciated by its creditors, and built a reputation of credibility in the world's financial centers.

Total debt in 1801 amounted to $81,996,268.49 and payments were made to reduce the debt to $74,728,023.98 at the end of 1803. The Louisiana Purchase added $15 million to Federal debt, but in spite of this, payments were made in 1804 to reduce the debt to $85,349,744.35. Debt reduction payments in 1805, 1806, and 1807 reduced the debt to $67,727,756.76.

Such prompt payments built a reputation in the eyes of the nation's domestic creditors that strengthened the financial operations of the government. The strong performance of the country helped to position it in the world community of nations. The country was able to complete the Louisiana Purchase and still reduce its debt by over $14 million. The purchase provided a vast area of land to increase the power and advancement of this new fledgling nation.

The National debt at the end of 1815 stood at a little over $127 million, but in peace-time conditions the government continued to pay off debt, so that by 1829 the debt was only slightly less than $50 million.

When Andrew Jackson was inaugurated in 1829, he established a strict policy to drive the debt down to zero, and by 1834 he announced that his policy had succeeded. His State of the Union Message to the Congress that year declared that the Treasury would discharge all outstanding Federal Debt and by January 1, 1835, the treasury would have a positive balance of $440,000.

In the total history of our country, and possibly in the history of any country, a zero debt government was unique. No country had ever repaid all of its outstanding debt. The debt-free environment did not have a very long life, since after Jackson left office, the country was thrown into a deep depression. Federal Revenues shrank to less than 50 per cent of those experienced in 1836 in the following year. The debt rose to $32 million and when the Mexican War was fought, debt rose to $68 million. In 1847 during the Mexican War Congress empowered the Treasury to pay all principal and interest on the debt when it came due—regardless of the amount paid out. While this empowerment might have saved the Congress the trouble of annually passing a specific bill to make such payments, it eventually led to Federal budgets running out of control.

After the Mexican War, during the peace and prosperity in the 1850's, the Federal Debt was reduced by 50 per cent. By 1857 a new depression hit, and the debt was continually increased so that by the end of 1860 it reached $68,844,000. The forces of depression caused the debt to rise to more than $524 million in the next year. Federal Expenditures exceeded Revenues by more than $1 million per day.

Significant expenditures during the war between the states made it necessary for the Congress to provide for the financing of those expenditures. Prior to 1864 there was never a necessity to consider an income tax to provide additional financing, but on June 30, 1864 the 38th Congress passed the first "duty on personal incomes."

Section 116 of that legislation provided, "That there shall be levied, collected and paid annually upon the gains, profits, and income of every person residing in the United States a duty of 5 per cent in excess of $600 to and including $5,000 and 10 per cent on incomes over $5,000." Any family was entitled to a deduction of $600, and all other taxes were deductible. Real estate gains were to be included in income, and real estate losses were to be deducted from income.

This duty on incomes was to be abolished by 1871, but the Congress allowed the duty to be collected in 1872, and the law was repealed in 1873.

Almost all writers have led us to believe that there was no income tax until after the passage of the XVI Amendment to the Constitution—passed by the House and the Senate in 1909, but not ratified by the States until February 1913. We will consider the XVI Amendment as the BEGINNING—the beginning of the perilous route of tax and spend, tax and spend that has led our country into its current state of continuing Federal Deficits, and ever increasing Federal debt.

In spite of the passage of an "Income Tax"—really labeled a "Duty on all incomes from whatever source," Federal Expenditures in 1862 were 8.13 times Federal Revenues, While revenues before the war reached a maximum of $74 million, by 1866 the Federal Debt reached $2,755,764,000. But peace-time allowed the government to reduce debt.

As before, the government paid off debt every year without fail until 1894, when the severe depression of the 1890's hit, and at that time the debt had been reduced by two-thirds.

During World War I Federal Debt rose to 20 times the level before the war, and again, after the war debt was reduced by two-thirds. Andrew Mellon, then Secretary of the Treasury, stated two principles: **"One is the balancing of the budget, and the other is the payment of the public debt. Both are in line with the fundamental policy of the government since its beginning."**

A man named John Maynard Keynes was largely responsible for vast changes in United States government fiscal policy. What a tragedy that he was so convincing to his economist colleagues, because of his outstanding command of the English language, since his theories of economics are seriously flawed. His theories are inadequate and useless in predicting real world events. Information on the state of the economy is always too late to be useful in such predictions. His thesis that in good times taxes must be increased and spending must be cut appears to be politically impossible. While depressions are easily recognized, the prosperous times are never, never truly understood when they occur. Keynes' theory of "reduce taxes in bad times and increase government spending, regardless of the debt created," has become total economic insanity. His idea of "increase taxes and reduce spending in good times to provide government surpluses" is unattainable in the real political arena. The problem is, what taxes should be increased to create more revenue, and an example of a non-revenue producing tax was the "luxury tax in 1990" expected by government economists to produce $16 million the next year only raised $58,000! Most economists inherently have such a lag in their proposed controls, that it is like driving an automobile with controls that do not respond to your actions until several hours, days or months after you took action. It's no wonder our country is in trouble. Keynes also said that government debt doesn't matter—what a total heresy—debt does matter as we have come to realize. The 1995 controversy between the administration and the leaders of Congress, which led to the shut down of many government activities, is a national and international disgrace. Not only did the President and the Congress conspire to shoot down the balanced budget Constitutional Amendment, an amendment to force the Congress and the Administration to do what they should be doing if they were properly carrying out their respective responsibilities, but they engaged in political bickering from the fiscal year-end in October, until after the start of 1996. What totally irresponsible actions by individuals given the responsibility to govern the country by the suffering electorate. The leaders are part of the many who didn't care.

The so-called "Balanced Budget Controversy" was over a possible continuing set of Federal Deficits that would drive our total Federal Debt as high as $7.5 trillion by the year 2002!

The controversy was futile because neither party to the fight realized that the most important change in National Tax Policy was a set of changes to improve the investment climate, and to improve the national savings rate of individuals. All the changes proposed were too little and too late.

## *Investment in Great Britain from 1760 to 1860*

Economists studied the level of total investment in Great Britain starting in 1760 and did such a study in ten-year increments from 1761 through 1860. They found that total investment rose from eight Million pounds sterling per annum in the 1761–70 decade, to fifty-eight million per annum in the 1851–60 decade.

As a per cent of Gross Domestic Product the level increased from 8 per cent to 14 per cent, a significant increase over the 100 years. In assessing the growth of Gross Domestic Product, in the first decade, 1761–70, GDP grew at a rate of only slightly over 0.5 per cent per annum. By the last decade, 1851–60, GDP grew at a 2.8 per cent per annum rate. The results indicate that real economic growth is vitally tied to the investment ratio—imagine an increase in the investment ratio from 8 per cent per annum to 14 per cent per annum brought with it a 5.6 times increase in the rate of real economic growth!

Those studies strongly support the premise that real economic growth is driven by the level of investment. The data are clear—this is not empty economic theory—this represents economic FACTS.

It must be remembered that Great Britain was totally contained in the British Isles a bounded and limited land mass. In contrast the United States in those same years was a growing nation continually increasing its land area, and its population. The U.S. needed much more investment to expand its boundaries, and to provide products for its ever-growing population.

According to the Encyclopedia Americana the population of the Americas in 1800 totaled 10 million and by 1938 had reached 255 million, the greatest growth on any continent. Such population growth brought with it a corresponding expansion in investment and increases in real economic growth.

By 1860 the United States had grown to a land stretching from the Atlantic ocean to a line running due North and South west of Iowa and Missouri. By 1890 the frontier stretched from the Canadian Border through the Dakotas and the largest part of Colorado on into Texas. In 1869 the East-West railroad was opened to traffic and the frontier eventually became the Pacific Ocean. A nation was born, bred and raised.

The driving spirit that led the Pilgrims and other persecuted people to sail across the Atlantic to establish new colonies which eventually became States continued to drive settlers West in search of peace to be free and to carve a homeland out of what many considered The Great American Desert. Those pioneers conquered that desert and with hard work and determination developed those lands into the greatest corn and wheat producing areas in the world. Eventually the same pioneering spirit drove the United States to its preeminent position as the world's leading producer and military and diplomatic power. That position in the world started to decline immediately after the Tax Reform Act of 1969 was passed and signed into law by Richard M. Nixon.

You will see in the pages that follow the critical detrimental effects of the tax laws of 1969, 1976, and 1986. You will also see the changes that are proposed to turn around our country and to get it moving on a path to create more jobs, more new technology, new products, faster real economic growth, balanced Federal budgets, and reduced Federal debt. With these new policies our international trade balance will also be brought into its proper posture.

**"Consumption is the sole and end purpose of all Production."** Adam Smith.

Commenting on the economic legislation of Medieval England, in 1805 David Macpherson wrote, **"From the perusal of most ancient statutes relating to commerce, manufactures, fisheries, and navigation, it is evident that the legislators knew nothing of the affairs which they undertook to regulate."** It is apparent that throughout history that same malady afflicts almost all Congresses, and indeed almost all government agencies involved in regulatory activities.

In New York 1930, Sir John Clapham at Cambridge set forth: **"Every economic historian should have acquired what may be called the statistical sense, the habit of asking in relation to any institution, policy, group, or movement the questions: How large? How long? How often? How representative?"**

What I have found is that many economists utilize time spans, some times ten years, sometimes centuries, often overlooking critical events shaping the activities of people. The daily activities of people are critical to the economic performance of nations. The daily decision to invest rather than to consume can mean the difference between strong economic growth or flagging economy.

Professor J. R. Hale in 1971 stated, **"The governments of Renaissance Europe as being paralyzed by economic and statistical ignorance and an almost total lack of skilled, experienced administrators. Economic policies rested on guesswork—most of it wrong."**

In 1972, Davis, Sterling, and Parker estimated the growth in U.S. Net National Capital Formation from 1805–1900. For the first thirty-five years, the level hovered between 6.2 and 7.0 per cent of

NNP. By 1889–98 the level peaked at 19.7 per cent and between 1894–1903 fell back to 18.4 per cent. There certainly was a significant increase in the importance of capital as one of the components of economic growth. During those years the United States was growing in area as well as population, entire States were being admitted to the new country, vast land areas were acquired along with the people living on those lands. In that period there was a tremendous surge of economic growth.

The combination of vast land areas and policies that caused the investment ratio to reach as high as 19.7 per cent prior to 1898, were essential to the growth of the United States as a world power. That power was not manifested until the war for the Preservation of Democracy, World War I. The powerful German war machine was brought to its knees by the tremendous productive power of the United States. Not only men but machines provided the balance of power necessary to win the war.

The study of the 100-year economic history of Great Britain indicated that real economic growth was only 0.5 per cent per year when the investment ratio was about 8.0 per cent. It could be concluded that at an investment ratio of about 7.0 per cent there would be no economic growth at all, only replacement of plant and equipment and no creation of new products, and new technology, or new jobs.

It appears that each one-per cent increase in the investment ratio would cause an increase in economic growth of about 0.4 per cent, based upon the experience of Great Britain.

Somewhat parallel experience is observed when the decade of 1950 to 1960 is studied. Real economic growth was about 3.34 per cent per year and the investment ratio was near 18 per cent in the United States. Real economic growth fell to only 1.599 per cent from 1990 to 1993, and the investment ratio fell to 13.98 per cent.

Both United States and Great Britain history of economic performance certainly indicate that if a country wishes to improve its real economic growth it must motivate its citizens to have the courage to invest in the future of the country to create new jobs, new products, new technology, and improved productivity.

The serious problem in the United States of continuing Federal Deficits, and burgeoning Federal debt, while it has been exacerbated by continued out of control spending, has really been caused by low real economic growth. In the last 20 years Federal revenues have held steadily at levels of about 22 to 23 per cent of Gross Domestic Product, and if that level of revenues had held over the last 20 years, it is evident that the real problem is that with low investment ratios, real economic growth has been much too low. Fostering higher real economic growth by improving the investment climate for individuals so that more individuals will have the courage to take a risk and create new jobs, new products, and new technology, and improved productivity is possible by simplifying the tax laws, and providing for either rollover of capital gains tax deferred, or by reducing the tax on capital gains to between 10 and 11 per cent as pointed out in analytical studies as the rate at which total tax revenues are maximized.

The nation's problem is real and threatening but the solutions to the serious problem are straight-forward and possible. Tax policy must be radically changed to motivate individuals to save and invest rather than to consume. Both Great Britain and United States economic history clearly shows that increased investment causes increased economic growth, and the last 50 year history of the United States shows that tax revenues are relatively constant as a per cent of Gross Domestic Product. The road to more tax revenues is paved with more real economic growth—that proposition is indisputable. Significantly lower capital gains tax rates and or rollover of long-term capital gains could be an essential part of any changes in U.S. tax policies. Such changes would motivate individuals to have the courage to invest and take risks to create more new technology, new jobs, improved productivity, and much higher real economic growth. Real economic growth will inherently produce more revenues to balance the Federal budget and provide surpluses so that the country can pay down some of its horrendous debt.

Even though positive changes were made in the Internal Revenue Code in the 1978 to 1980 time period, and some progress was made, that progress was short lived. In 1986 the House and the Senate passed the Tax Reform Act Of 1986 which eventually was even worse than the 1969–1976 reform acts. Congress forgot about Alexander Hamilton.

Hamilton relied heavily upon writings of Emmerich de Vattel, one of the leading theorists of international law. That is, "natural Law" and the "Law of Nations." Hamilton following Vattel believed that there were three ends of government: providing for the great purposes of commerce, revenue, and agriculture; facilitating domestic tranquillity and happiness; and establishing sufficient stability and strength to make us respectable abroad.

We can learn a lot from that great American, and where we have lost sight of some of the principles which he held to be so important to the proper operation of government, we have caused considerable stress among the people of our country. That stress has been manifested in the formation of "militias" across our country which have been formed to defend the rights of some citizens who believe that the present government is not taking the right direction in a lot of its laws, judicial decisions, and financial management of our country.

Hamilton believed that a "Wise Government" would arrange its administration so that people at large were at liberty to follow the passions of private ambition and avarice—were expected and encouraged to do so—so that what they eventually did would necessarily contribute to the welfare of the republic. His idea was to reward people for honesty and diligence in pursuing their interests, and in time those people would indeed become more virtuous.

He also believed that natural inequalities among men would give rise to unequal distribution of wealth in any free society in which industry was encouraged. The rich and the poor, the few and the many, were natural antagonists. If all power were given to the few, they would oppress the many; if all power were given to the many, they would oppress the few. His idea was to give the few and the many each a separate branch of government, believing that neither would dare neglect to participate actively in the affairs of the nation, lest its natural enemy gain full control of power.

Hamilton also foresaw a possible corruption of the government he envisaged and believed that a President chosen for a limited term of years would continuously be looking forward to reelection, and that even the best would be driven by their interests to abuse their power in order to be reelected. This is one aspect of both Representative and Senator problems; the subjugation of the future good of the nation to the necessity to be sure to get reelected. Such problems have led to the perception that many of the legislators didn't care. They didn't care enough about the total welfare of the country to do the right thing for the country because it would endanger their reelection. This drive to satisfy the many so that reelection is assured is really a departure from the concepts of a balance of power between the few and the many. Remember the words of Alexander Tyler, **"the majority always votes for the candidate promising the most benefits from the public treasury—with the result that democracy collapses over a loose fiscal policy, always to be followed by a dictatorship."**

CHAPTER THREE

# A Leadership Trip to Washington, D.C. Motivates a Concerned Citizen

## *A Concerned Citizen*

In January of 1976 the author was a member of a leadership trip to Washington, DC by the Greater Los Angeles Chamber of Commerce. On this trip the Directors of the Chamber meet with leaders in our National Government. Cabinet members including the Secretaries of all Departments, leaders of Congress including Chairmen of Congressional Committees, The President, and finally the Chairman of the Federal Reserve were all on the itinerary.

Almost all of the meetings were educational and informational, however, several were memorable and were instrumental in inciting the author to study further and to gather information and facts to arrive at an understanding of the critical problems faced by our country because of the total ignorance of the Congress and the Administrations concerning the financial welfare of our country. Hopefully it is not ignorance, but rather that they didn't care, they certainly didn't care enough to do anything to right the wrongs which had been done to ruin the investment climate in our country that has led to our current precarious condition of horrendous Federal Debt, Continuing Federal Deficits, low economic growth and unacceptable unemployment.

Most outstanding of all the meetings was the meeting with Chairman Al Ulmann of the Ways and Means Committee of the House of Representatives. After his presentation, the author asked this question, "Mr. Ulmann as chairman of the second most powerful committee of the Congress, are you going to be able to provide the leadership to change our tax laws to improve the investment climate for our country's individuals?"

His answer, "No, no, no."

The author's further question, "If you can't who is supposed to provide the leadership?"

His answer,"You are, you are."

The author's response, "Damn it, you asked for it and you are going to get it!"

That interchange goaded the author into vowing to do something about our country's terrible condition. But later in our meetings with President Ford he referred to the tax law of 1976 as "a good bill." It was then that the author knew our country was in deep trouble: the President didn't even know what trouble our country was in! That comment made the author even more motivated to do something.

The last meeting of the day was in the Board Room of the Federal Reserve with the then chairman the well-regarded Dr. Arthur Burns. Dr. Burns spoke to our group of eighteen for about twenty minutes. As he finished, he asked our Chief of Mission Albert C. Martin the noted architect, are there any questions? Mr. Martin then said to the author, "OK Ballhaus tell him!"

At the time the author had with him a Hewlett Packard Computer. He showed it to Dr. Burns and said, "Dr. Burns, I checked with the manufacturer of this product and the cost of labor increased 31 per cent, and the cost of materials increased 23 per cent, yet the price four years ago was $400 and now in spite of the increased cost of labor and materials the price is only $100—how is this possible? The only way this is possible is the company must have invested to bring the cost of the product down so that it could be sold for $100.

Investment drives the cost of the product down, investment increases productivity, investment increases economic growth."

The author pointed to the charts on the walls of the Federal Reserve Board Room and said, "Dr. Burns your charts indicate that since 1969 inflation has grown from 3 per cent to 13 per cent, productivity has dropped from over 3 per cent to just over 1 per cent per year, Real Economic Growth has dropped from over 4 per cent to just over 1 per cent per year, interest rates have rocketed from 5 per cent to 15 per cent, and unemployment has shot from 3 per cent to 10 per cent. Why is that? The 1969 tax law has fouled up our investment climate and people have stopped investing in the future of their country. Investment creates productivity, enhances economic growth, creates jobs, fights inflation, provides capital as equity rather than debt and thereby reduces interest rates. What we need is changes in the tax laws to improve the investment climate in our country to motivate individuals to invest in the future of their country."

Dr. Burns retorted, "Young man, I want you to shout that message in all the halls of Congress, and I want you to continue to shout that message, because you are absolutely right!"

The author answered, "Sir, with a response like that, from a man like you in a position like yours, I won't quit!"

As a result of the admonitions of Dr. Arthur Burns, the author spent the next year studying the reports of the Senate Finance Committee, the House of Representatives Way and Means Committee, and the Joint Congressional Economic Committee. The reports of these committees indicated that none of these bodies was aware of the serious conditions which existed and the serious trends of conditions that were continuing. These committees seemed oblivious to the serious nature of the economic trends. In the six years since the passage of the Tax Reform Act of 1969 the following trends and conditions existed:

> Total Government Receipts had grown from 187 Billion to 356 Billion by 1977, a 90.3 per cent increase. From a Surplus of 3.2 Billion in 1969, deficits grew to a total of 53.6 Billion by 1977.

Total Federal Debt grew from 367 Billion in 1969 to 709 Billion by 1977, a 92.3 per cent increase.

In spite of these serious trends in economic performance, the Congress apparently didn't care. The most important issue was "be sure to get reelected." National competitiveness in world markets continued to deteriorate, unemployment soared, interest rates shot to new highs of 15 per cent, inflation had reached as high as 13 per cent. But they didn't care.

The United States of America with the most productive people, with unbounded resources, and with abundant space to grow, was reduced to a second rate economic power, all by tax laws that penalized investment and saving, and motivated consumption by individuals. A comparison with Germany and Japan indicates some very interesting differences. Differences that truly have influenced the relative economic performance of these three countries. Remember that Japan has almost no natural resources, and certainly no excess space to grow, yet their performance over the years since that nation was totally defeated in World War II, has been incredible. It is estimated that by the end of 1996 Japan's Gross National Product will exceed that of the United States. There are reasons for this. Japanese people save four times as much as Americans, and Japanese industry invests twice as much as United States industry.

CHAPTER FOUR

# A Concerned Citizen's Campaign

## *The Campaign*

After the leadership trip to Washington DC in 1976, the author was motivated to start a campaign to change the investment climate for individuals in the United States. After spending a year studying the reports of the House Ways and Means Committee, the Senate Finance Committee, and the Joint Economic Committee, the author was convinced that there was no understanding or no knowledge by the Congress of the terrible problems that had arisen as a result of the tax law of 1969 and later the tax law of 1976.

President Nixon had signed into law the Tax Reform Act of 1969, and President Ford had signed into law the Tax Revenue Act of 1976, and neither one of these presidents really understood what a terrible law was made effective by their signatures. They should have vetoed both bills if they had proper staff work by their subordinates. But no one was intelligent enough to realize that the country would eventually be in serious trouble if those two laws were made effective.

The Tax Reform Act of 1969 had several provisions that made the investment by individuals significantly more difficult, and even noxious because of several provisions such as: If you invest and win your taxes will be almost doubled; if you invest and lose you can only write off half your losses; and if you borrow money to make an investment, you cannot deduct all of the interest paid on those borrowings. Therefore, these three provisions made it much more difficult to take a risk with the possibility of losing, even if you win having your taxes doubled, and preventing you from deducting all of the interest paid on borrowings made to permit further investment. The obvious increase in the risk-to-reward ratio fouled up the investment climate for individuals to such an extent that individuals shunned investment and started to consume rather than invest. That critical decision by millions of individuals—to consume rather than invest led to the serious decline of the United States as a world economic power, a serious increase in negative international trade balances, continuing Federal Deficits, high unemployment, high interest rates, higher than usual inflation rates, and lagging industrial productivity. No foreign military action has done as much to ruin the status of the United States as a World Economic Power as the tax laws of 1969 and 1976. The results are clear, they are unmistakable, they are indisputable. No economic theory, no guessing games on the outcome are needed, the facts and the data are real. Continuing Federal Deficits, burgeoning Federal Debt are the results of tax laws that curtailed investment and motivated consumption.

Early in 1977 Dean Harold L. Williams of the University of California at Los Angeles Graduate School of Business hosted a breakfast for a number of business leaders to meet with Senator Edmund Muskie who at the time was chairman of the Joint Economic Committee of the Congress. When it was time for Senator Muskie to talk, the first words out of his mouth were, "Since industry has been unable to provide the jobs needed by our ever-growing labor force ..." The author stood up and waved his arms attempting to stop the Senator but he continued to talk and the author continued to wave his arms until the Senator stopped and with a perturbed tone of voice asked, "Well what's your problem?"

The author said, "Senator Muskie, you said, 'Since industry has been unable to provide the jobs needed by our ever-growing labor force ...' may I point out to you that the Congress has passed tax laws which have fouled up our investment climate for individuals that has led to less investment which has caused high unemployment, low economic growth, low productivity growth, higher interest rates, higher inflation, and severe negative balances of international trade." "Industry's hands and feet are tied by these unfavorable tax laws, if you will do something to untie our hands and feet we will provide so many jobs we will have over-employment just like Germany where they are importing Turks, Jugoslavs and Greeks to man their ever-increasing work force. "We will improve our international competitiveness, improve our real growth, drive prices down and fight inflation, and will increase tax revenues so that the country can pay its bills, balance the Federal Budget, and pay off some of our continually increasing Federal Debt."

Senator Muskie responded by saying, "You must come and see me in Washington!" At that point Dean Williams said, "Don't worry Senator, he'll be there!" The rest of the meeting was spent informing the members of the group about the actions that can be taken in Washington. There were interesting exchanges between the business leaders and the Senator who was serious about his chairmanship of this very important committee of the Congress. Later the author was able to visit the Senator in Washington, and the Senator set up a meeting between the author and his staff: the result was the Joint Economic Committee Report arrived at a consensus of all members of the committee. That is the first time in its history that a consensus was reported by this committee. The consensus was that policies should be changed to improve the climate for investment. WE NEED MORE INVESTMENT!

The campaign was started in January 1977. The author produced a brochure entitled, *How To Put 4,000,000 Americans Back To Work Without Raising Taxes*. The first contact was made with the author's Congressman, Charles Wiggins. The author showed Mr. Wiggins the brochures and after a brief reading by Mr. Wiggins, he asked, "What are you trying to accomplish?" The author said, "I'm going to get a reduction in the tax on capital gains." To which Mr. Wiggins replied, "I've been here for twelve years, and haven't been able to get a damned thing done. You think you as a private citizen can get a program through the Congress?" A quick reply by the author, "Yes because I intend to see all members of the House Ways and Means Committee, all members of the Senate Finance Committee, the Secretary of Commerce, the Assistant Secretary of the Treasury for Tax Policy, and any other people who can be effective in changing the tax law." Wiggins asked where and how did you get all the appointments to see all these people?" The author said, "I got them by telephone from California. After all, I am President of Beckman Instruments, Inc., President of the California Chamber of Commerce, Vice Chairman of the National Association of Manufacturers, a Director of the United States Chamber of Commerce, and a member of the tax committees of those organizations."

Mr. Wiggins wished me luck in my pursuit of the changes so important to our country's future.

After I left his office I visited all members of the Ways and Means Committee, all members of the Senate Finance Committee, The Secretary of Commerce, and the Assistant Secretary of the Treasury for Tax Policy, and the response from all these individuals was so positive that the author was motivated to prepare a Supplement I to the original brochure. The Supplement I was published in February of 1977 and contained more information concerning the sad state of the nation's economy, and proposals to change the tax laws to improve the nation's investment climate.

Responses from Carl Curtis of the Senate Finance Committee and his colleague, Cliff Hanson, were most supportive of my campaign. Two members of the Ways and Means Committee spent some time with the author, and those two members, William Steiger and Jimmy Jones listened in a joint meeting with the author and were convinced that something must be done and they jointly sponsored the Steiger-Jones Bill which eliminated the minimum tax on long term capital gains. That Bill reduced the tax on long term capital gains from a high of 49.125 per cent to 35 per cent. That Bill passed with flying colors and was the first in a number of changes that started to improve the investment climate for individuals.

Later in briefings to Russell Long, then Chairman of the Senate Finance Committee, he listened intently and after the fourth meeting he said, "I have believed in the things you are talking about, over the years, but I have never seen the concepts put into such clear language and into such convincing charts; I'm going to help you!"

In meetings with the Joint Tax Committee, Russell Long, who was chairman, asked, "Why not restore the 70 per cent deduction for all long term capital gains," and when a cry against such a proposal went up, he said, "Well I'll settle for 60." And that is how the tax on long term capital gains was further reduced to 28 per cent.

Later, when the tax on all income was reduced to 50 per cent, the tax on long term capital gains was reduced to 20 per cent. The nation responded by increasing the amount of investment by individuals over the next few years. Productivity started to improve, economic growth increased, unemployment started to decline, and the country started to regain its economic strength. Inflation abated, interest rates fell, and the international trade balance started to improve.

The improvement was short-lived, because in 1986 the Congress passed a bill that would undo all the good things that the previous tax laws had created. The 1986 tax law was even worse than the 1969 and 1976 tax laws. Those laws were signed by Presidents Nixon and Ford, and guess what? The 1986 tax law was signed into law by President Reagan—certainly as a result of bad advice by his staff—because President Reagan in principle would never have signed such a bill if he had been given the total story of the negative effects such a bill would have on the economy of the country. Almost all of the bad effects were hidden in the provisions of the law. Imagine a 648 per cent increase in your capital gains tax—or a 150 per cent increase in your tax if you were in the $20,000 income bracket. Obviously the Congress did not know that they were causing such outrageous changes in the tax on long term capital gains of people at the lower levels of income.

There were some good provisions of the bill but they were overshadowed by the horrendous changes to the capital gains tax. Excerpts from a letter sent to all members of the Senate Finance Committee follows:

## *Excerpts from a Letter to Senators*

On June 19, 1987 the author sent a letter to all members of the Senate Committee on Finance.

"There are two significant provisions (of the Tax Reform Act of 1986) which have serious negative effects on the personal, private investment climate, and if history and experience can tell us anything, can have a profound negative effect on the overall economic well-being of our country.

"A direct comparison of the 1969 and 1986 increases in the tax on long term capital gains shows that the 1986 Act is appreciably worse than the 1969 Act, especially in its effect on lower income individuals.

"... for individuals with low or no income the tax on a $20,000 capital gain increased 648 per cent under the 1986 Act and 0 per cent under the 1969 Act! With other taxable incomes as high as $40,000 that same $20,000 gain is taxed over 100 per cent higher under the 1986 Act and 0 per cent under the 1969 Act. Such terrible taxation of capital gains under the 1986 Act will eventually have a negative effect on the personal, private investment climate.

"These increases in rates will not produce more revenue and will certainly severely injure the economy. Studies have shown that a top long term capital gain tax rate of 11 to 13 per cent will maximize tax revenues.

"The proper solution to this serious problem is to re-enact Section 1202(a) the 60 per cent deduction for long term capital gains, and Section 1222(3) the six month holding period. These two provisions would set the maximum tax rate on capital gains at between 11.2 and 13.2 per cent. Such a change would maximize tax revenues and stimulate vitally needed investment to drive real economic growth, improve productivity, provide sorely needed new jobs for ever expanding work forces, and regain our competitive posture in world markets.

"The tremendous job of hammering out a 1986 Tax Reform Act is behind us and no changes should be made. The two changes suggested will not change any other elements of the Act, but would serve our country well by motivating vitally needed personal, private investment to power our industrial machine.

"May I have your views on the suggested changes? I will be happy to work with your staff to submit a bill for consideration by The Committee on Ways and Means and the Senate Finance Committee."

The sum of their responses were polite, somewhat interested, but did not commit to any action to improve the tax law to benefit the personal, private investment climate and eventually the total economic performance of the country. Needless to say the changes were never enacted and our country continued to suffer Federal Budget deficits, and a continually growing Federal debt. The Federal Debt now stands at $5 trillion an incomprehensible amount. What is even more incomprehensible is the fact that the House and the Senate do not care that the Federal Debt has reached such lofty heights—heights that make eventual reduction or pay-off almost impossible—and with no plan to reduce deficits and no plan to pay down the debt.

The responses to the letter sent to the Senate Finance Committee from some of the Committee members showed no understanding of the severe negative effects on the investment climate for individuals. Most of the responses were not really responsive to the analysis presented in the letter. Most of the responses were almost apologetic for the actions taken, but in sum those actions were all for the good of the country, in their opinions. History will show how wrong most of the members of the Committee were in defending their actions. The 1986 tax law undid all of the good things that several tax laws subsequent to 1977 had accomplished. Viewing only two economic measures—The Federal Deficit and the Federal Debt will lead to some simple conclusions. Listed below are the annual Federal Deficits and the Year-End Federal Debt:

| Year | Federal Deficit | Federal Debt | Annual Per Cent Increase in Deficits |
|---|---|---|---|
| 1987 | 149,769,000,000 | 2,345,578,000,000 | 10.64 |
| 1988 | 155,187,000,000 | 2,600,760,000,000 | 10.88 |
| 1989 | 152,481,000,000 | 2,867,538,000,000 | 10.25 |
| 1990 | 221,354,000,000 | 3,206,207,000,000 | 11.81 |
| 1991 | 269,521,000,000 | 3,598,303,000,000 | 12.23 |
| 1992 | 290,403,000,000 | 4,001,941,000,000 | 11.22 |
| 1993 | 254,670,000,000 | 4,351,223,000,000 | 8.73 |
| 1994 | 234,758,000,000 | 4,676,029,000,000 | 10.94 |
| 1995 | | | |

One simple conclusion is that there was not sufficient personal, private investment to create the economic growth necessary to provide the tax revenues to cover our ever-increasing Federal Expenditures. A 50-year study of tax revenues collected showed that the per cent of taxes collected varied from 19 to 22 per cent of Gross National Product. In other words, if you want to increase tax revenues you must create **real economic growth!** One other simple conclusion is that the tax law became so complicated and complex that such complication and complexity made it much more difficult for an individual to make investment decisions. Reduced investment means lower rate of economic growth.

Could it be that the Committee members didn't care? Certainly if the Committee staff had made an analysis similar to the one presented in the letter to the Committee, most Committee members would not have knowingly passed such a horrible law. While the 1986 Tax Law did do some good things as indicated in my letter to the Committee, those good provisions were over-shadowed by the negative impact on the investment climate for individuals.

## *Predictions of Future Federal Debt (1977)*

During the author's 1977 campaign to reduce tax rates on long term capital gains, he studied the possible scenarios and their effect on the annual Federal Deficits and the corresponding effect on Federal debt.

It was pointed out that if total tax receipts and total Federal expenditures were to continue at the same rates of growth that existed in the years 1970 to 1976, the annual Federal Deficit would grow to $217 billion by 1982, and the corresponding Federal Debt would reach $1.53 billion.

Since the country had experienced better rates of growth in tax receipts and expenditures in the 1965 to 1970 period, it was assumed that with no changes in the tax law, the government could control operations, at least, to maintain the same rates of growth as then existed. With such a scenario, budget deficits would grow to 140 billion and the debt would rise to $1.3 trillion.

If the total receipts were to grow as experienced in the 1965 to 1970 period, but expenditures were to be held to the same per cent of Gross National Product as had been experienced in the 1965 to 1970 period, by 1982 the predicted deficit would be reduced to $30 billion.

None of these possible scenarios, as difficult as they might be to control, would lead to the President's goal of a balanced budget by 1981. Without some significant change in the personal, private investment climate, the President's goal was obviously "pie in the sky."

The author fought hard to convince Congress and the Senate to make changes in the tax laws to improve the personal private investment climate. Several bills were introduced to improve the personal, private investment climate. The first bill provided for the creation of Individual Investment Accounts—similar to Individual Retirement Accounts, but without the deduction for tax purposes of any contributions to the account. In such an account all dividends, interest, and capital gains would accrue tax free so long as they remained in the account. Whenever anything was taken from the account full taxes would be paid on such a distribution. That bill did not pass.

The second bill provided for the "rollover of all capital gains tax free" (really tax deferred) so long as the proceeds from any sale of assets were completely re-invested within a one-year period. That bill did not pass.

The third bill eventually became the Steiger-Jones Amendment and eliminated the preference tax associated with long term capital gains—that provision reduced the maximum rate on long term capital gains from 49.125 per cent to 35 per cent.

The fourth bill was the re-instatement of the 60 per cent deduction associated with long term capital gain income. That Provision reduced the maximum tax rate on long-term capital gains from 35 per cent to 28 per cent.

Later when the maximum tax rate on all income was reduced to 50 per cent, the tax rate on long term capital gains was automatically reduced to 20 per cent. That rate prevailed until the infamous tax bill of 1986 undid all the favorable changes which had been made in 1978 through 1981. The capital gains tax rate for low level taxpayers was increased as much as 640 per cent, and for medium level taxpayers the tax rate was increased over 150 per cent—what a horrible unintended result!

In 1978 and again in 1980 Congress passed laws which reduced the rate of tax on capital gains to 28 and 20 per cent, respectively. Those significant changes drove inflation down from 13 per cent to as low as 3 to 4 per cent, interest rates fell from 21 per cent to as low as 7 to 8 per cent, unemployment dropped from 10 per cent to 7 per cent, and national productivity and international competitiveness started to improve.

In 1984 tax laws were passed that started to move in the opposite direction: investment decisions were made more difficult with the enactment of the complex alternative minimum tax. In July of 1986 the Senate passed a bill that instituted sweeping changes. Most of the changes were excellent: reduced individual tax rates, removing many lower level income groups from the tax rolls, and other clarifications in the tax code, but increasing the rate of tax on capital gains was, as Senator Alan Cranston declared on the floor of the Senate, "is total economic insanity!"

Remembering the powerful "pressure to invest" concept, the Senate was in the process of reducing the pressure to invest on individuals to 1.0—compared to the pressure to invest as high as 8.33 in the period 1960 to 1969.

Capital gains "rollover" is a simple change that would have truly powerful effects on the investment decisions of individuals. If an investor sells an asset and re-invests the total proceeds of the sale, there is no tax, but if he re-invests none of the proceeds of the sale, he would pay the full tax, and if he re-invests only half of the proceeds he would pay one-half the tax on the gain.

Rollover would free up all the capital in the country, and provide complete mobility of capital, and with that provide for the maximum utility and effectiveness of the country's capital stock. Rollover would motivate individuals to remain as investors and would eventually cause a significant increase in the number of investors. Remember investors are the "good guys" and we should have more of them if we want our country to grow and to prosper as a powerful economic force in the world's family of nations.

The tragedy of taxing capital gains is manifested in the **reduction of the nation's capital stock**, when the government taxes capital gains those taxes are forever lost to the capital stock of the nation, in other words, the capital taxed away becomes funds for spending or consumption by the government.

Some simple computations will illustrate the point:

1. If an investor has $10,000 to invest and receives a return of 20 per cent per year, in 15 years his capital has increased to $154,070 with no sale of assets with or without rollover.
2. If that same investor sells and re-invests the proceeds each year for 15 years, with rollover his total capital would be $154,070, just as before.
3. If that same investor sells and pays a 28 per cent tax each year on his gains, in 15 years his capital would increase to $75,230. In other words the investor's capital has been decreased by over one-half if he must pay a 28 per cent tax on his gains. That is a terrible loss in the capital stock of our country!

When the government taxes away capital it is killing the goose that lays the golden eggs! Investment capital creates jobs, improves productivity, creates national wealth and higher standards of living. Investment capital drives the cost of products and services down.

CHAPTER FIVE

# Views of Our World Class Competitors

**"Where destiny blunders, human prudence will not avail"**
—Publilius Syrus

When the author first visited Japan the Japanese Yen was traded at 360 Yen to the U.S. Dollar. In the years following his first visit there was not much change in the relative value of the Yen and the Dollar. After the passage of the Tax Reform Act of 1969, there was a substantial change in the personal private investment climate in the United States, and the subsequent lack of investment led to significantly reduced economic growth, and worst of all tremendous negative trends in the balance of trade between the U.S. and Japan.

Over a long period of years the Japanese people have saved and invested between three and four times the amount of investment and saving by U.S. people. That difference in relative investment and saving has permitted the Japanese economy to grow at a rate such that it approaches the total U.S. economy.

On April 19, 1995 the powerful Yen had reached an all-time high against the US Dollar at a rate of 79.75 Yen per Dollar. Even more important, the strong Yen when presented in terms of total economic strength of the Japanese economy, indicated that the total gross domestic product of Japan had reached within two-tenths percentage points of equalling the total gross domestic product of the United States!

Futurologist Herman Kahn had predicted in the early sixties that the Japanese economy would surpass that of the U.S. by the early 21st century, it was quite a shock to some of Kahn's detractors, who-had greeted his original predictions with scorn. Those detractors did not realize how powerful our tax laws had been to inhibit savings and investment by our people. Certainly they had not understood the power of the savings and investment of the Japanese people, and the power of compound interest and compound growth in the economy over a long period of years. With the Japanese investing as much as 27 per cent of their gross national product and the U.S. investing 14 per cent, the growth in productivity in Japan was at a level three times that of the U.S. over a long period of years. Japan economic growth has proceeded at a rate almost twice that of the U.S. At such rates of growth it is no wonder that the Japanese economy will eventually exceed that of the U.S. Japanese tax policy has largely been responsible for motivating the Japanese to save and invest, and Japanese industry to invest heavily, the results are clear. Investment is the power behind the tremendous surge in the Japanese economic power throughout the world.

If the economic power of the United States is to be regained, we need changes in our tax laws to motivate our people to save and invest. As the laws now stand there is only confusion and uncertainty, and such confusion and uncertainty make it almost impossible for people to take the risk and make the critical decision to invest. Uncertainty is the largest deterrent to investment, but lack of adequate after tax return on any investment is also an important deterrent to investment. The needed tax changes will remove uncertainties, and provide significant improvements in after-tax returns to investors.

In 1985 the Yen was worth 240 to the Dollar and the Japanese economy was only one third the size of the U.S. economy, but by the year 1994 they advanced to a Gross National Product as high as 83 per cent of the U.S. economy—and the Yen reached 83.95.

One Japanese investment manager observed that, Japan with one-half the population and one twenty-fifth the land area, it is preposterous that the Japanese could stand shoulder to shoulder with the United States in economic terms. Many American economists feel that the Yen's current surge has bloated the statistical size of the Japanese economy far beyond its real strength. Even McDonalds realized that the prices of their hamburgers were exorbitant because of the rise in the value of the Yen, so they cut their prices by as much as 38 per cent.

Even at home the Japanese people found that they really needed 181 Yen to buy what an American could buy at home for $1. This is moderated by the fact that Japanese workers today earn much more than U.S. workers, mostly because of the high investment rates that spurred productivity growth which in turn allowed the payment of higher wages to workers. Of course, Japanese people can take advantage of the high value of the Yen when they travel overseas, and when they invest overseas.

Many Japanese believe that the relative strength of the Yen in the world against the Dollar is really due to the decline in the U.S. economy rather then a sign of their own country's economic power. With our horrible tax policy which motivates consumption rather than investment, there is no doubt that the U.S. has declined with respect to the whole world not just the Japanese Yen.

McDonalds' president, Den Fujita, suggested that if the Japanese government fails to take bold measures to open Japan's markets to imports, and to bring down the trade surplus, the Yen could advance to as high as 50 Yen to the Dollar by 1999. If that did happen Japan's gross domestic product would become 1.4 times that of the United States.

A country only half the size of the United States in population terms, its industries such as steel, semi-conductors, and automobiles meet or exceed those of the U.S. and their shipbuilding actually dwarfs that of the U.S. On May 3, 1995 an editorial In the Asahi newspaper cited, "The relative decline of the American economy, is symbolized by the ceaseless fall in the value of the Dollar. It is even losing the status of a nation whose currency serves as an international standard of exchange."

Japan is not only growing in economic power, but is now the world's largest aid donor and is the nation with the largest pool of savings in the world. What more evidence do we need to convince us that Japan's tax policy has fostered investment, savings, and growth, while that of the United States fosters consumption, and ignores the importance of saving and investment.

The tax law of 1954 was a step in the right direction, but the 1969, 1976, and 1986 tax laws have all made it difficult for the personal private investor by reducing the after-tax return on investment and introducing provisions that lead to significant uncertainty all of which have ruined the personal private investment climate.

## *A European Banker's Opinion*

In early May of 1995 the head of Germany's central bank, in his most pointed remarks to date on the prospects for the beleaguered dollar, said it would not rise against the Japanese Yen or the German Mark until the markets were convinced that President Clinton and Congress were taking steps to reduce the United States' declining savings rate and reduce the Federal Budget Deficit.

"The problems for me are clear," said Hans Tietmeyer[2], the president of the reserve bank, widely known as the Bundesbank. "Low savings ratio, relatively high budget deficit, no absolute assurance that it will come down in the long run, and a high net debtor position on the part of the United States. These are the points that have to be addressed.

"It is not only the presence of the current deficit that seems to concern the markets, but also the prospect for the future. The markets seem to think that there is not enough correction on the way, as far as these fundamentals are concerned. The markets of today are more and more looking to the future, more than just the present."

Mr. Tietmeyer was not shy in criticizing the United States for making little progress in finding a long term solution to bringing down future deficits.

Others in Europe blame the weak dollar for dragging down other currencies like the French franc, Italian lira, and Spanish peseta.

Tietmeyer also said, "I am not interested in interfering in the policy of the United States, I am only saying that it is important to understand what are the problems behind the dollar's low value, and that the markets are not only looking at the present problems but they are looking always at what will happen in the future."

He also said several times, "Every country has to take care of its own currency, and a strong dollar was in the best interest of the United States as well as the rest of the world, since most nations stored their excess cash in dollars.

He said, "Vital to the United States reducing its debt would be the promotion of higher savings by Americans. Americans save only 4 per cent of the Gross National Product, compared with 12 per cent in Germany, and 17 per cent in Japan. Because of such a low savings rate, the United States is dependent upon foreigners buying its debt paper, and thus is more subject to swings in market sentiment.

"While the Administration is convinced that there should be a strong dollar, and has said as much, the markets are looking at what policy decisions are behind those words."

CHAPTER SIX

# "The Beginning" A Condensed History of Income Tax Legislation

### *Before the Beginning*

The author thought that our story should start at the "Beginning," that is, the beginning of the tax on incomes of individuals, as provided by the XVI Amendment to the Constitution. Additional research led the author to believe that everyone would be intrigued by the early systems of providing revenue to finance the operations of the country.

The first Congress financed the operations of the United States by placing duties on all items of commerce being imported into the country, and by levying a tonnage tax on all ships. The total receipts were $4,399,473.09 from customs and $19,440.10 in miscellaneous income. That income was not sufficient to cover operations of the government, so $5,791,112.56 was borrowed by the Treasury.

By 1800 customs receipts were $9,080,932.73, and with other small revenues, required borrowing was reduced to only $1.602 million. By 1803 revenues exceeded $10 million and no borrowing was required.

In 1804 the Louisiana Purchase required the Treasury to borrow an additional $15 million, driving the total Federal Debt to $85,349,744.35. Except for that transaction, every year subsequent to 1801 debt was reduced by the government, and after that purchase, debt was reduced from the above level to $67,727,756.76 by the end of 1807.

The important lesson to be learned from this early history of the economic performance of our fledgling nation, is that during peace-time the Congress had the fiscal responsibility to continually reduce total Federal debt. Certainly our current Congress could learn that fiscal responsibility is imperative if we are going to survive. It is difficult to find where the precept, "debt doesn't matter" was born and raised. It does matter as you will see in the pages that follow.

While everyone believes that the United States did not have a tax on personal income prior to 1913, the author found that during the Civil War—The War Between The States—the damn Yankees did enact an income tax to finance the expenditures necessitated by the operations of a war machine. The tax was short-lived but did exist until 1873.

Congress did try to create an income tax law in 1894, but the Supreme Court ruled it unconstitutional in the year it was enacted —the XVI Amendment is still considered the "Beginning" of our downfall and you will see the terrible events and economic performances that have been put in play by the complex, complicated and almost impossible to understand Internal Revenue Code as it is today. The Internal Revenue Code was very moral until the Tax Reform Act of 1969, and has fallen into deeper and ever deeper disrepute with the 1976 and 1986 versions of the Internal Revenue Code. Don't blame the people in Internal Revenue Service, blame the Congress.

The Congress has played and played with the laws of our country regarding income taxes, making significant changes almost every year. It seems that they will never get it right. The purpose of this book is to make clear what the right tax policies are and how to achieve those right policies. The nation cries out for positive changes that will not have to be changed again for many years. The positive tax policies of 1954 to 1969 are proof that it can be done, and we must see that it is done.

> **"As it was in the beginning, is now, and ever shall be, taxes without end, Amen."**

## *"The Beginning"*

On February 25, 1913 Philander C. Knox, Secretary of State of the United States of America executed a valid Article XVI of the Constitution of the United States:

"The Congress shall have the power to lay and collect taxes on incomes, from whatever source derived, without apportionment among the several States, and without regard to any census or enumeration."

It was less than 8 months before the first act was passed as HR 3321 by the first Session of the 63rd Congress on October 3, 1913 as Chapter 16:

> An act to reduce tariff duties and to provide revenue for the Government, and for other purposes.

That was the first law which motivated citizens to consume rather than invest, because it lowered prices of imported goods, and made it easier for importers to sell their goods at lower prices to the consumer. That law taxed incomes and capital gains at the same rates; there was no distinction between income from investment and other types of income. The entire legislation was contained in a total of 14 pages.

Section II A subdivision 1 provided for a flat tax of one per cent of all income of every citizen, and subdivision 2 provided for an additional tax:

1 per cent between 20,000 and 50,000
2 per cent between 50,000 and 75,000
3 per cent between 75,000 and 100,000
4 per cent between 100,000 and 250,000
5 per cent between 250,000 and 500,000
6 per cent for incomes above 500,000

The law provided for annual returns to be filed for the previous year, but provided for an exemption of $4,000 for each individual. It also provided for a Deputy Commissioner at $4,000 per year and two division heads at $2,500 per year.

For comparison purposes computations will be made for taxable incomes of 10,000; 50,000; 100;000; 500,000; 1,000,000; and higher levels where appropriate. The original tax law of 1913 resulted in the following taxes at various levels of income:

| Taxable Income | Normal Tax | Surtax | Total Tax | Per Cent |
|---|---|---|---|---|
| 10,000 | 100 | 0 | 100 | 1.000 |
| 50,000 | 500 | 300 | 800 | 1.600 |
| 100,000 | 1,000 | 1,550 | 2,550 | 2.550 |
| 500,000 | 5,000 | 20,050 | 25,050 | 5.010 |
| 1,000,000 | 10,000 | 50,050 | 60,050 | 6.005 |
| | | | 60,050 + 7% | |

There appeared to be no public outcry against the 1913 law which reduced tariff duties and replaced the lost revenue from such reductions with revenues collected directly from individuals and corporations. Such legislation permitted importers to sell their products at reduced prices to United States consumers and increase the importers' share of markets. Such a law obviously improved international trade between the United States and its trading partners, and such a law should have increased the sales of imported products to US consumers. Since there was no serious objection to the tax law of 1913, the Congress later found an almost unbelievable source of continually increasing revenue—The Income Tax!

The next tax law was passed in 1916 on September 8th as HR 16763. It was, "An act to increase the revenue, and for other purposes."

The Congress certainly had found an almost ideal source of new revenues, revenues which would permit ever-growing Federal Expenditures.

Revenues were almost doubled by the passage of the 1916 tax law and rates at all levels were increased substantially. Computations of taxes at various levels of income are presented below:

| Taxable Income | Normal Tax | Surtax | Total Tax | Per Cent |
|---|---|---|---|---|
| 10,000 | 200 | 0 | 200 | 2.0 |
| 50,000 | 1,000 | 400 | 1,400 | 2.8 |
| 100,000 | 2,000 | 2,000 | 4,000 | 4.0 |
| 500,000 | 10,000 | 33,000 | 43,000 | 8.6 |
| 1,000,000 | 20,000 | 83,000 | 103,000 | 10.3 |
| 2,000,000 | 40,000 | 198,000 | 238,000 | 11.9 |
| above | | | 238,000 + 13% | |

A comparison of tax levels at similar incomes shows that, at the lower levels of income, taxes were doubled, while at the highest they were only increased by 83 per cent. Certainly total Federal Revenues from the individual income tax were increased nearly 100 per cent.

Congress must have been very happy to be able to double taxes for individuals without causing any serious repercussions during times of relative peace. But a terrible war was going on in Europe. Most Americans are not familiar with the history of the First World War.

Wars are almost always fought over important issues, although they are sometimes started by rather insignificant happenings. The direct cause of the war was the ultimatum given by Germany to Russia on August 1, 1914. That ultimatum changed a local quarrel between powerful Germany and relatively weak Russia into an eventual worldwide conflict. From a political standpoint the insignificant happening was the assassination of the Austrian Archduke Franz Ferdinand and his wife at Sarajevo on June 28, 1914. While this act was an excuse to take action to start a war, statesmen and soldiers had been expecting and preparing for war over the years.

After Germany's unification in 1871, the excellent educational system, the technical training and scientific research, and the outstanding skilful labor and economic production methods enabled

Germany to flood the markets of the world with their wares. They were supreme in chemical industries, and in shipbuilding they were the equal of Great Britain. Their financial standing was of the highest, and German capital stood behind powerful enterprises. Their ships ploughed the Seven Seas. Germany had the industrial and commercial strength to conquer the world without firing a shot. At the same time the German Army was considered to be the most efficient and largest fighting machine in the world. The German Navy was second only to the British Navy. Germans settled the continents of the world and their banks had branches in almost every country, and German commercial activities were evident on all continents.

Such outstanding prosperity led to ambitions and aspirations which looked far beyond the artificial frontiers and boundaries that encompassed this powerful nation. German leaders of thought expounded the gospel of force, the idea of the survival of the fittest, and the natural predominance of the strong over the weak. Trietschke had described war as "drastic medicine of the human race" and banishing war was not only meaningless but "immoral." He also expressed contempt for the "tottering British Empire."

As early as 1900 The "Koloniale Zeitschrift" had stated, "The old century saw a German Europe, the new one will see a German World." The Kaiser proclaimed at Bremen, "God has called us to civilize the World." Field Marshal Bronssart von Schellendorf stated "—hence we intend to absorb one after another all the provinces which neighbor on Prussia. We will successively annex Denmark, Holland, Belgium, Northern Switzerland, and then Trieste and Venice; finally, Northern France from the Sambre to the Loire."

Britain had seen German enterprise invade all the markets of the British Empire. The United Kingdom itself was flooded with products marked "Made in Germany." The British continued to buy German goods because they needed them and the goods were then cheaper or not at all available from British manufacturers. The pressures were building on both sides, pressures that eventually would erupt into World War I.

On July 28, 1914 Austria declared war on Serbia, on August 1, 1914, Germany declared war on Russia, and two days later on France.

On August 4, 1914 Great Britain declared war on Germany. Every nation declared war on every other nation, but the surprise was that Japan declared war on Germany on August 23, 1914.

The extent of the war was greater than any American can imagine. There were several Fronts: the Western Front, the Eastern Front, the Southern Front, the Colonial and Turkish Campaigns, and Naval and Air Operations. This was truly a World War of immense magnitude. The conflagration by 1918 involved 93 per cent of the world's population, 130 million were neutral, 1.7 billion were involved and participated in the war. The objective of Germany to rule the world by force of arms led to the description of that war as a War to Preserve Democracy. By 1917 it became clear that the United States would become involved, and on April 6 the United States declared war on Germany.

With such a tremendous obligation to provide men, armaments, ships and aircraft to our allies, the United States was forced to pass a tax law that would provide the revenues to be able to pay for all the costs of a total war. The Congress met its responsibility as required by passing the "War Income Tax" on October 3, 1917. The 65th Congress Chapter 63 created, "An act to provide revenue to defray war expenses, and for other purposes."

One of the first provisions of the law was the reduction of the personal exemption from $4,000 to $2,000, so that all individuals had their taxable income increased by $2,000, which means all individuals had a slight increase in their tax obligation. The law was different than previous laws because the "War Income Tax" was an addition to taxes levied under the previous schedule of rates.

**WAR INCOME TAX**

| Taxable Income | 1916 Tax | War Tax | Total Tax | Per Cent |
|---|---|---|---|---|
| 10,000 | 200 | 275 | 475 | 4.750 |
| 50,000 | 1,400 | 3,900 | 4,300 | 8.600 |
| 100,000 | 4,000 | 12,300 | 16,300 | 16.300 |
| 500,000 | 43,000 | 149,800 | 192,800 | 38.560 |
| 1,000,000 | 103,000 | 372,300 | 475,300 | 47.530 |
| 2,000,000 | 238,000 | 892,300 | 1,130,300 | 56.515 |
| above | | | 1,130,300 + 65% | |

There is no doubt that the Congress was forced to act decisively to increase revenues to cover the extensive expenses necessary to prosecute the all-out war effort not only for the United States itself, but also for the support of all the allies with added food, material, transport, and consumer products as well as war supplies.

Even with the significantly increased revenues, the demands of the total war effort forced the country to borrow extensively to be in a position to pay all the required bills. To minimize the cost of borrowing, the treasury sold war bonds at relatively low interest rates to finance the high rates of expenditure necessitated by the total war effort.

The world heaved a sigh of relief when the Armistice was signed on November 11, 1918. Even so it took many months to bring all hostilities to a full conclusion. On November 25, 1918 the last remnant of the German forces in East Africa surrendered.

In spite of the reduction in financial requirements as a result of the cessation of hostilities, the Congress in 1919 passed a tax increase for the year 1918 but a slight tax reduction for the year 1919. The 65th Congress in Session III Chapter 18 on February 24, 1919 three months after the end of hostilities, passed "An act to provide revenue, and for other purposes." The Revenue Act of 1918. The normal tax was increased to 6 per cent of incomes below $4,000 and 12 per cent of incomes above $4,000. In addition there was a surtax ranging from 1 per cent at $5,000 to 65 per cent over $1,000,000. The computations are presented below:

**FOR THE YEAR 1918**

| Taxable Income | Normal Tax | Surtax | Total Tax | Per Cent |
|---|---|---|---|---|
| 10,000 | 960 | 110 | 1,070 | 10.700 |
| 50,000 | 5,760 | 5,510 | 11,270 | 22.540 |
| 100,000 | 11,760 | 23,510 | 35,270 | 35.270 |
| 500,000 | 59,760 | 263,510 | 323,270 | 64.654 |
| 1,000,000 | 119,760 | 583,510 | 703,270 | 70.327 |
| above | | | 703,270 + 77% | |

The Congress was very magnanimous in 1919 because they did reduce the Normal Tax from 6 per cent of $4,000 to 4 per cent, and from 12 per cent to 8 per cent for incomes over $4,000. As you can see the reductions were very small:

| Taxable Income | Normal Tax | Surtax | Total Tax | Per Cent |
|---|---|---|---|---|
| 10,000 | 640 | 110 | 750 | 7.500 |
| 50,000 | 3,840 | 5,510 | 9,350 | 18.700 |
| 100,000 | 7,840 | 23,510 | 31,350 | 31.350 |
| 500,000 | 39,840 | 263,510 | 303,350 | 60.670 |
| 1,000,000 | 79,840 | 583,510 | 663,350 | 66.335 |
| above | | | 663,350 + 73% | |

At the lowest levels of income 1919 taxes were reduced by about 30 per cent, while at the highest levels the reduction amounted to only 5.68 per cent. Evidently the Congress was intent on maintaining a rather large amount of progressivity in the tax rates. Later Congress realized that such high tax rates in times of peace were considered to be rather confiscatory and some changes were made.

It wasn't until 1921 that the 67th Congress in Chapter 136 passed "An act to reduce and equalize taxation, to provide revenue, and for other purposes." The law was titled, "The Revenue Act of 1921." The Normal tax was not changed from the provisions of the law passed in 1919, however, the top rate was reduced from 73 to 58 per cent, but not until the tax year 1922. Actually there was almost no change to the level of taxes paid in 1921, but there was a significant change in the treatment of long term capital gains. For the first time in history the Congress finally realized the difference between gains realized as a result of risk-taking capital investments and other types of income such as wages, interest, dividends, or rents. Even that Congress seemed to understand that investment creates jobs, increases productivity, increases economic growth, and provides capital for industrial expansion. The treatment of long term capital gains was most interesting. Long term capital gains were subtracted from total income and were taxed at a fixed rate of 12 1/2 per cent of the gain, if taxable income was such that income would be taxed at higher than 12 1/2 per cent. Long term capital losses were treated in a very interesting manner: Taxes were to be computed on all income without subtracting the capital loss, and then deducting from computed taxes 12 1/2 per cent of the total net long term capital loss from the computed taxes. The regular tax computations-under the provisions of 1921 and 1922 are presented below:

**1921**

| Taxable Income | Normal Tax | Surtax | Total Tax | Per Cent |
|---|---|---|---|---|
| 10,000 | 640 | 110 | 750 | 7.500 |
| 50,000 | 3,840 | 5,510 | 9,350 | 18.700 |
| 100,000 | 7,840 | 23,510 | 31,350 | 31.350 |
| 500,000 | 39,840 | 263,510 | 303,350 | 60.670 |
| 1,000,000 | 79,840 | 583,510 | 663,350 | 66.335 |
| above | | | 663,350 + 73% | |

**1922**

| Taxable Income | Normal Tax | Surtax | Total Tax | Per Cent |
|---|---|---|---|---|
| 10,000 | 640 | 40 | 680 | 6.80 |
| 50,000 | 3,840 | 4,960 | 8,800 | 17.60 |
| 100,000 | 7,840 | 22,460 | 30,300 | 30.30 |
| 500,000 | 39,840 | 220,960 | 260,800 | 52.16 |
| 1,000,000 | 79,840 | 470,960 | 550,800 | 55.08 |
| above | | | 550,800 + 58% | |

It is evident that the reductions in taxes at the lowest levels were relatively small amounting to about 9.3 per cent, while at the highest levels the reductions were as high as 16.97 per cent. The important provision added to the tax code was the recognition of the difference between long term capital gains and other forms of income. Later we will see how important that provision of tax law will become as the country grew and prospered—and how terribly important that provision or the lack of knowledge of the effects of that provision will become paramount in causing the eventual decline of the economic power of the United States of America. Over the years the Congress made special conditions for taxing the long-term capital gains of individuals, and treated such gains in a number of different ways. We will trace the history of tax laws and,specifically the treatment of long term capital gains, over the years.

The 68th Congress Session I Chapter 234 passed the "Revenue Act of 1924" on June 2, 1924 an "Act to reduce and equalize taxation, to provide revenue, and for other purposes." This act finally did reduce the rate of taxation on individuals. The computations of taxes at various levels of taxable income are presented below:

| Taxable Income | Normal Tax | Surtax | Total Tax | Per Cent |
|---|---|---|---|---|
| 10,000 | 360 | 0 | 360 | 3.600 |
| 50,000 | 2,760 | 3,540 | 6,300 | 6.300 |
| 100,000 | 5,760 | 17,020 | 22,780 | 22.780 |
| 500,000 | 29,760 | 170,020 | 199,780 | 39.956 |
| 1,000,000 | 59,760 | 417,020 | 476,780 | 47.678 |
| above | | | 476,780 + 46% | |

Reductions of taxes to all individuals were considerable, and at the lowest levels amounted to 52 per cent, but at the highest levels reductions amounted to only 13.5 per cent. Congress still was intent on preserving the progressivity of the rates of tax—that is, high rates at high levels of income. The good part of the law was the recognition of the difference between gains from investment and other types of income such as dividends, interest, rents, wages, salaries, and fees. You will see in the pages that follow the serious impact of that provision of tax law, and how it has serious effects on productivity, real economic growth, taxes collected, unemployment, and interest rates, as well as balance of international trade.

The 1924 Act preserved the difference between capital gains and other ordinary income with a maximum rate of 12 1/2 per cent and the provision for capital losses by allowing a tax reduction amounting to 12 1/2 per cent of any net capital losses from an individual's tax.

The 1926 69th Congress on February 26,1926 passed the "Revenue Act of 1926" An act to reduce and equalize taxation, to provide revenue, and for other purposes." The law preserved the treatment of capital gains as in the 1924 act, but made significant reductions in normal and surtax rates. Computations of individual taxes at various levels of income are presented below:

| Taxable Income | Normal Tax | Surtax | Total Tax | Per Cent |
|---|---|---|---|---|
| 10,000 | 300 | 0 | 300 | 3.00 |
| 50,000 | 2,300 | 2,980 | 5,280 | 10.56 |
| 100,000 | 4,800 | 11,660 | 16,460 | 16.46 |
| 500,000 | 24,800 | 91,660 | 116,460 | 23.29 |
| 1,000,000 | 49,800 | 191,660 | 241,460 | 24.15 |

The new tax law made gigantic reductions in the taxes to be paid by individuals. At the lowest levels of income, the reductions amounted to 33.3 per cent, and at the highest levels the reductions amounted to 49.4 per cent. The 1926 act truly was a reduction in the level of taxation for individuals consistent with the considerable reductions in spending required for defense. Again the treatment of long term capital gains was as provided in the 1924 law. The 1928 Congress, the 70th Congress Session I Chapter 852 passed a new law on May 29, 1928. This was "An act to reduce and equalize taxation, provide revenues, and for other purposes." Titled "The Revenue Act of 1928," the law continued to treat long term capital gains as in the 1924 law. But what was touted as an act to reduce taxation actually decreased the normal tax at the lowest levels from 2 per cent to 1 1/2 per cent on incomes between 0 and 4,000, but held the tax rates from 4,000 to 8,000 at 3 per cent and at levels above 8,000 the rate of normal tax was held to 5 per cent. Computations of taxes at various levels of income are presented below:

| Taxable Income | Normal Tax | Surtax | Total Tax | Per Cent |
|---|---|---|---|---|
| 10,000 | 280 | 0 | 280 | 2.800 |
| 50,000 | 2,280 | 2,980 | 5,260 | 10.520 |
| 100,000 | 4,780 | 11,660 | 16,440 | 16.440 |
| 500,000 | 24,780 | 91,660 | 116,440 | 23.238 |
| 1,000,000 | 49,780 | 191,660 | 241,440 | 24.144 |
| above | | | 241,440 + 25% | |

Actually taxes were not measurably reduced at all. The law was a subterfuge and meant very little to the citizens who had to pay income taxes at any level of income. It would be interesting to find whether the House and the Senate took any credit for the act to "reduce and equalize taxation" when there was no reduction in taxes of any significant magnitude.

The 71st Congress in Session II Chapter 2 passed a joint resolution: "Joint resolution reducing rates of income tax for the calendar year 1929." The surtax was the same as in the 1928 tax law but the Normal Tax was reduced from 1 1/2 per cent on the first 4,000 of income to 1/2 per cent and for income between 4,000 and 8,000 the rate was reduced from 3 per cent to 2 per cent, and at incomes above 8,000 the rate was reduced from 5 per cent to 4 per cent. The surtax rates were held at the same levels as in the 1928 law. Computations of taxes at various levels of taxable income are presented below:

| Taxable Income | Normal Tax | Surtax | Total Tax | Per Cent |
|---|---|---|---|---|
| 10,000 | 180 | 0 | 180 | 1.800 |
| 50,000 | 1,780 | 2,980 | 4,760 | 9.520 |
| 100,000 | 3,780 | 11,660 | 15,440 | 15.440 |
| 500,000 | 19,780 | 91,660 | 111,440 | 22.288 |
| 1,000,000 | 39,780 | 191,660 | 231,440 | 23.144 |
| above | | | 231,440 + 24% | |

The result of that resolution by Congress was the reduction of normal tax rates so that the reductions at the lowest levels of income were 35.7 per cent and at the highest levels of income the reductions amounted to only 4.2 per cent. The Congress still maintained a significant amount of progressivity in tax rates at the highest levels of income.

## *Financial Performance in the 1920'S*

By 1921 the country had a surplus of $36,892,271.61 and made some progress in reducing the total Federal debt. In 1923 the surplus was $309,557,460.30 and further reduced the Federal debt. In 1925 the country experienced a surplus of $250,505,238.33 and reduced the Federal Debt even further. In 1926 the surplus was even higher at $377,767,816.64. By 1928 the surplus increased to a high of $398,828,281.06. In 1929 the surplus was reduced to as low as $184,787,035.42. Imagine the year after year reduction in the total Federal Debt, at a time that the country was recovering from the effects of a terrible World War. The United States had provided the production of food and military material to supply the Allies sufficient equipment and men to destroy the German military machine. To accomplish this great task the United States had to borrow many billions of dollars in the 1917 through 1919 years.

Taxes were increased sharply to provide some of the funds to cover the costs of such a tremendous effort, but taxes were not sufficient and Federal borrowing rose to unheard of heights in the nation's history. The War effort quickly led to the emergence of the U.S. as a real world power. What was important, was the continuing effort to reduce the total Federal Debt, in the years following the war. In those days peacetime was a time to reduce debt, and serious efforts were made to establish a program to create continuing surpluses, which made possible the payoff of debt. The country was following the precepts of Alexander Hamilton—the country should pay its debts and build integrity and sound credit-worthiness. The country was building integrity in the community of nations. Such sound actions would be important in advancing the reputation of the U.S. as a world power.

By 1931 the country started to experience deficits $481.3 millions growing each year to 2,735.3; 2,601.6; 3,629.6; 3,001.8; 4,360.6; and 2,707.4 millions in the 1932 through 1937 years, respectively. Total Gross Public Debt rose from $16.8 billion in 1931 to $36.4 billion by 1937. Total Public Debt had grown at a rate of almost 14 per cent per year. That was the start of continuing growth of the

Federal debt. Since this time the country has never been out of debt, and now the debt has risen to almost $5 trillion! This is our nation's most pressing problem, but almost nobody seems to care! Almost all the world's leading nations over the past have fallen because of the horrible financial management of their governments. Government debt allowed to grow to unmanageable proportions has led all the failing countries to plunge into despair and disrepute.

The self-imposed discipline of Alexander Hamilton to force the country to meet its obligations and to build its reputation for integrity was being disregarded in the 1930's and ever since then the country has accepted the rationale that debt does not matter. The day of reckoning is not too far in the future. Actions must be taken soon to reverse the trend of tax and spend, but worst of all to spend even that which the country does not have—but borrow to meet all the needs of the government—regardless of the consequences. Later you will see the policies which have led to the present situation, and hopefully, you will see the actions that need to be taken to reverse the destructive trends now prevailing in our country. The proposed actions are simple and straightforward, yet powerful in the results to be obtained. Now is the time for positive action to be taken, it will never be too late but it could be too little, unless total actions are taken.

In 1932 the 72nd Congress in Session I Chapter 209 passed a law on June 6, "An act to provide revenue, equalize taxation, and for other purposes." The act was titled, "Revenue Act of 1932." HR 10236

The act preserved the provisions for treating long term capital gains in the same manner as the previous laws, but there was a significant increase in taxes at all levels of income. Computations of taxes at various levels of income are presented below:

| Taxable Income | Normal Tax | Surtax | Total Tax | Per Cent |
|---|---|---|---|---|
| 10,000 | 640 | 40 | 680 | 6.80 |
| 50,000 | 3,840 | 4,690 | 3,530 | 17.06 |
| 100,000 | 7,840 | 22,460 | 30,300 | 30.30 |
| 500,000 | 39,840 | 223,560 | 263,800 | 52.76 |
| 1,000,000 | 79,840 | 491,460 | 571,300 | 57.13 |
| above | | | 571,300 + 63% | |

Compared to the 1929 law the new law increased taxes at all levels of income. At the lowest levels taxes increased as much as 397 per cent!

At the highest levels of income, taxes were increased 247 per cent. Such increases in the tax burden of individuals certainly had some really horrendous effects on the economic performance of the United States. We will see the effects on the economy in studies conducted later in this treatise. The only good provisions of the law were the treatment of long term capital gains. The maximum tax on capital gains was held at 12 1/2 per cent.

The 73rd Congress in Session II Chapter 277 made significant new approaches to the taxation of long term capital gains. For assets held for less than one year capital gains were taxed the same as ordinary income. For assets held less than 2 years gains were taxed at 80 per cent as ordinary income. For assets held more than two years and less than five years gains were taxed at 60 per cent of the net gain. For assets held for more than five years and less than ten years 40 per cent of the gain was taxed, and for assets held for more than 10 years 30 per of the gain was taxed as ordinary income. These provisions were truly a change in philosophy or understanding of the nature of long term capital gains and their taxability. The normal tax was simplified to a simple 4 per cent of all income and the Surtax ranged from zero below 4,000 to 59 per cent above 1,000,000. Computations of taxes at various levels of income are presented below:

| Taxable Income | Normal Tax | Surtax | Total Tax | Per Cent |
|---|---|---|---|---|
| 10,000 | 400 | 300 | 700 | 7.00 |
| 50,000 | 2,000 | 7,700 | 9,700 | 19.40 |
| 100,000 | 4,000 | 28,000 | 32,000 | 32.00 |
| 500,000 | 20,000 | 245,500 | 265,500 | 53.10 |
| 1,000,000 | 40,000 | 533,000 | 573,000 | 57.30 |
| above | | | 573,000 + 63% | |

Taxes were increased only slightly at all levels of income, but the treatment of long term capital gain was changed considerably. Also the tax philosophy of treating long term capital gains was changed.

This represented a new approach to handling risk-taking by individuals—the benefits of holding investments for long terms were obvious—and the incentive to make long term investments was clear. This was a step in the right direction. Long term investment is most beneficial to the over-all performance of the economy of any country. Investment provides capital to permit companies to grow, creates new jobs, new products, increases the over-all productivity, improves the international trade balance, and stimulates real economic growth—the result is increased tax revenues to permit government to pay its bills and provide the services needed by its citizens. You will see in later studies how lack of investment in the United States led to continuing Federal Deficits, burgeoning Federal Debt, unfavorable international trade balances, weakening of the US Dollar, and much higher than desirable unemployment.

The above law was enacted on May 10, 1934 as "An act to provide revenue, equalize taxation, and for other purposes." Long term capital losses were allowed up to $2,000, HR 7835.

The 74th Congress in Session II Chapters 689–690 as HR 12395 passed the "Revenue Act of 1936" on June 22, 1936. Long term capital gains and losses were treated the same as the 1934 law. The Normal Tax was held at 4 per cent, but the Surtax was considerably increased at higher levels of income. Computations of taxes at various levels of income are presented below:

| Taxable Income | Normal Tax | Surtax | Total Tax | Per Cent |
|---|---|---|---|---|
| 10,000 | 400 | 300 | 700 | 7.00 |
| 50,000 | 2,000 | 7,700 | 9,700 | 19.40 |
| 100,000 | 4,000 | 30,000 | 34,000 | 34.00 |
| 500,000 | 20,000 | 286,000 | 306,000 | 61.20 |
| 1,000,000 | 40,000 | 641,000 | 681,000 | 68.10 |
| 2,000,000 | 80,000 | 1,371,000 | 1,451,000 | 72.55 |
| 5,000,000 | 200,000 | 3,591,000 | 3,791,000 | 75.82 |
| above | | | 3,791,000 + 79% | |

The 1936 law was the first time tax rates as high as 79 per cent were seen in any tax law to that date. Long term capital gains were again treated the same as in previous acts.

The 75th Congress in Session III Chapter 289 made some changes in the treatment of long term capital gains and losses. Long term gains were to be taxed at a maximum rate of 30 per cent, and there was a capital loss allowed of $2,000, but also the tax was computed as the tax on ordinary income and reduced by 30 per cent of the net capital loss. Again the Congress appeared to understand that risk-taking and gains from such risk-taking were different than other types of income. The 1938 law was passed on May 28, 1938, "The Revenue Act of 1938." or HR 9682. Computations of taxes at various levels of income are presented below:

| Taxable Income | Normal Tax | Surtax | Total Tax | Per Cent |
|---|---|---|---|---|
| 10,000 | 400 | 300 | 700 | 7.00 |
| 50,000 | 2,000 | 7,700 | 9,700 | 19.40 |
| 100,000 | 4,000 | 30,000 | 34,000 | 34.00 |
| 500,000 | 20,000 | 286,000 | 306,000 | 61.20 |
| 1,000,000 | 40,000 | 641,000 | 681,000 | 68.10 |
| 2,000,000 | 80,000 | 1,371,000 | 1,451,000 | 72.55 |
| 5,000,000 | 200,000 | 3,591,000 | 3,791,000 | 73.82 |
| above | | | 3,791,000 + 79% | |

When comparison is made between the 1938 law and the 1936 law, the income tax on ordinary income was the same in both years, the significant change was in the treatment of long term capital gains.

In 1939 there was a sweeping change in the tax laws of the United States. Mr. Colin F. Stam and Mr. L. L. Stratton, members of the staff of the Joint Committee on Internal Revenue Taxation, working with the assistance of the Department of the Treasury and the Department of Justice, created the 1939 edition of the Codification of Internal Revenue Laws. That codification was enacted without change by the 76th Congress as HR 2762 on February 10, 1939.

A unanimously favorable report by the Ways and Means Committee carried the House of Representatives by 350 to 16 on January 25, 1939. The bill was then sent to the Senate Finance Committee on January 27, 1939. A unanimously favorable report by the Senate Committee on Finance on February 1, 1939 was sent to the full Senate and was passed in the Senate without a recorded vote.

One of the most sweeping changes involved the treatment of long term capital gains. A gain was treated as ordinary income if the holding period was less than 18 months. 66 2/3 of any net gain was considered to be ordinary income for holding periods from 18 to 24 months, and for holding periods of more than 24 months 50 per cent of the gain was taxed as ordinary income.

In addition there was an alternative maximum tax on long term capital gains amounting to 30-per cent of the net long term capital gain.

Long term capital losses were allowed a deduction in taxes of 30 per cent of the net long term capital loss. Ordinary tax rates were not increased over the 1938 law by any significant amount, but there was an earned income credit of 10 per cent of net incomes up to $14,000. Computations of taxes at various levels of income are listed below:

| Taxable Income | Normal Tax | Surtax | Total Tax | Per Cent |
|---|---|---|---|---|
| 10,000 | 400 | 300 | 700 | 7.00 |
| 50,000 | 2,000 | 7,700 | 9,700 | 19.40 |
| 100,000 | 4,000 | 30,000 | 34,000 | 34.00 |
| 500,000 | 20,000 | 286,000 | 306,000 | 61.20 |
| 1,000,000 | 40,000 | 641,000 | 681,000 | 68.10 |
| 2,000,000 | 80,000 | 1,371,000 | 1,451,000 | 72.55 |
| 5,000,000 | 200,000 | 3,591,000 | 3,791,000 | 73.82 |
| above | | | 3,791,000 + 79% | |

There was no meaningful change in the rates of taxes at various levels of income, but there was a recognition that long term capital gains were different than other types of income, and there was some recognition that earned income was somewhat different than dividends, interest, rents and other so-called "unearned income." This is the first time earned income was treated differently than other types of income. The rates of tax on long term capital gains ranged from a low of 2 per cent of any gain to as high as 30 per cent of any gain, when that gain is from an investment held for over 24 months, however, when an investment is held for 18 to 24 months the rates of tax ranged from 2.6667 per cent to 53 per cent, and for holding periods of less that 18 months, rates ranged from 4 per cent to 79 per cent. No provision was made for deduction of short term capital losses beyond any short term capital gains.

The 76th Congress on June 25, 1940 passed Public Act No. 1. "An act to provide for the national preparedness by raising revenue and issuing bonds, to provide a method of paying for such bonds, and for other purposes." In addition to the taxes computed under the Internal Revenue Code there was a "Defense Tax for Five Years" which provided that all taxpayers after December 31, 1939 shall add 10 per cent to all taxes computed under provisions of the Internal Revenue Code. Prior to adding the Defense Tax to the regular tax, the specified taxes on individuals are listed below:

| Taxable Income | Normal Tax | Surtax | Total Tax | Per Cent |
|---|---|---|---|---|
| 10,000 | 400 | 360 | 760 | 7.60 |
| 50,000 | 2,000 | 11,780 | 13,780 | 27.56 |
| 100,000 | 4,000 | 36,780 | 40,730 | 40.78 |
| 500,000 | 20,000 | 292,780 | 312,780 | 62.56 |
| 1,000,000 | 40,000 | 647,780 | 687,780 | 68.78 |
| 2,000,000 | 80,000 | 1,377,780 | 1,457,780 | 72.89 |
| 5,000,000 | 200,000 | 3,597,780 | 3,797,780 + 79% | 75.95 |

After December 31, 1939 all such taxes were increased by 10 per cent under Section 15 of the 1940 Tax Law.

The 77th Congress Session I Chapter 412 on September 20, 1941 passed the "Revenue Act of 1941." That act increased taxes at all levels of income and the taxes are computed at various levels of income below:

| Taxable Income | Normal Tax | Surtax | Total Tax | Per Cent |
|---|---|---|---|---|
| 10,000 | 400 | 1,320 | 1,720 | 17.20 |
| 50,000 | 2,000 | 19,380 | 21,380 | 42.76 |
| 100,000 | 4,000 | 49,780 | 53,780 | 53.78 |
| 500,000 | 20,000 | 325,230 | 346,280 | 69.25 |
| 1,000,000 | 40,000 | 693,780 | 733,780 | 73.38 |
| 2,000,000 | 80,000 | 1,443,780 | 1,523,780 | 76.18 |
| 5,000,000 | 200,000 | 3,723,780 | 3,923,780 +79% | 78.47 |

It can be seen that taxes at the lowest levels of income were increased appreciably, while at the highest levels the per cent increase was much smaller, mainly because there was almost no possibility of taking the same percentage increase at the highest levels, since a 366 per cent increase would have taken more than the total income of taxpayers at the highest levels.

The 77th Congress in Session II Chapter 619 on October 21, 1942 passed the "Revenue Act of 1942." Here again the taxes at the lowest levels of income were hit the hardest. With a Normal Tax of 6 per cent and a Surtax ranging from 13 per cent to 82 per cent the tax computations are listed below:

| Taxable Income | Normal Tax | Surtax | Total Tax | Per Cent |
|---|---|---|---|---|
| 10,000 | 600 | 2,020 | 2,620 | 26.20 |
| 50,000 | 3,000 | 23,240 | 25,240 | 52.48 |
| 100,000 | 6,000 | 59,140 | 65,140 | 65.14 |
| 500,000 | 30,000 | 385,140 | 415,140 | 83.03 |
| above | | | 415,140 + 88% | |

One most important provision of the 1942 Act was the realization that long term capital gains should be treated differently than other forms of income. The holding period to be considered "long term" was 6 months. Assets sold in less than 6 months had any net gain taxed as ordinary income, however, assets held for more than 6 months carried a 50 per cent deduction from the gain that was excluded from income so the range of rates on long term capital gains started at a low of 3 per cent and ended at a high of 44 per cent. Capital losses were limited to $1,000.

The 1942 act had a sneaky little provision providing for taxes to be withheld at a level of 5 per cent of salary or wages, but this was only a test balloon for the most insidious tax law of all—the withholding of all income taxes at the source of income passed in 1943. A man named Beardsley Rummell proposed to the Congress that the collection of income taxes would be speeded up and made more certain of collection, if taxes were collected as the income was earned, with the rates of withholding attempting to withhold the proper amount of taxes from each pay check for each individual.

Over-withholding, although a serious financial problem to individual taxpayers, resulted in the refund of over-withheld taxes after the end of the tax year being considered a "tax dividend" that became a palliative to many individuals who considered it pennies from heaven. Many taxpayers became oblivious to the level of taxes they were paying, because they never actually handled the taxes collected, and never realized the tremendous burden they were carrying. Most taxpayers would have been shocked to pay in one check on April 15th of each year the amount of taxes that had been quietly removed from their control each payroll period.

That devious method of tax collection of income taxes has led to the insensitivity of most taxpayers to the terrible state of our current tax laws, and the damage they have done to our national economy. Withholding rates have been raised and lowered over the years and will be treated in all the tax laws that follow.

While the first attempt at withholding was accomplished in the Revenue Act of 1942 at a rate of 5 per cent across the board, the 1943 Act provided for withholding rates varying from a low of 10 per cent to a high of 20 per cent for incomes over $200 per week.

The most complicated sections of the law provided for the extension of the exact date for paying taxes due on April 15, 1943 until September 1, 1943 so long as any interest due was also paid on that date It was obvious even to the Congress that 1943 would be a year when taxpayers would have to pay double taxes, those for the prior year, and those being collected through withholding. It required five pages of the law to explain these provisions.

## *The Most Insidious Tax Law of All*

The 78th Congress in Session I Chapter 120 on June 9, 1943 passed into law "An act to provide for the current payment of the individual income tax, and for other purposes." The act was titled "Current Tax Payment Act of 1943." The act provided for the collection of all wages and salary income tax at the source of earning. The insidious result was that taxpayers eventually did not know how much tax was being paid each year and in many cases even more taxes were withheld than were due, and the resulting refund made some people very happy to receive this unexpected tax "dividend."

Income taxes were collected in a very "painless manner" and the flow of taxes was an endless source of revenue to be spent as soon as it was received by the Government—the trouble is that the Government spent much more than they collected and had to borrow more than they collected, and they caused the Federal Debt to increase at an alarming rate; alarming to any thinking people, but not alarming to the Congress. The painless nature of the income tax collections rendered the Congress to become oblivious to complaints of the people about their tax burden, because there were not many complaints—most people did not feel the serious burden they were carrying and were happy to receive annual refunds of over-withheld taxes. Most people were not knowledgeable about the time value of money and did not realize that taxes withheld each week or month eliminated the interest that they could earn on that money if they had earned it, saved it, invested it, and then paid all of their taxes on April 15, after the close of the year. Withholding truly was an increase in each citizen's tax bill that was hidden from them.

The lack of realization of the burden of taxes on each citizen led to a lack of complaints by constituents to the Congress and that led to continuing irresponsible actions of Congress which has led to the nation's almost 5 trillion dollar debt.

The 78th Congress 2nd Session Chapter 210 passed HR 4646 on May 29, 1944. An act "To provide for simplification of the individual income tax." The act was titled, "Individual Income Tax Act of 1944."

The normal tax was at 3 per cent, and the surtax ranged from 20 per cent at the lowest levels of income to 91 per cent at the highest levels. Taxes computed at various levels of taxable income are listed below:

| Taxable Income | Normal Tax | Surtax | Total Tax | Per Cent |
|---|---|---|---|---|
| 10,000 | 300 | 2,640 | 2,940 | 29.40 |
| 50,000 | 1,500 | 26,820 | 28,320 | 56.64 |
| 100,000 | 3,000 | 67,320 | 70,320 | 70.32 |
| 500,000 | 15,000 | 429,820 | 444,820 | 88.96 |
| 1,000,000 | 30,000 | 884,820 | 914,820 | 91.48 |
| above | | | + 94% | |

It was nice of the Congress to put a limitation on the maximum tax any taxpayer could pay at 90 per cent of taxable income. Withholding maximum rate was at 22.5 per cent.

The 79th Congress 1st Session Chapter 453 passed HR on November 8, 1945. An act "To reduce taxation, and for other purposes." The act was titled, "Revenue Act of 1945."

The normal tax was at 3 per cent less 5 per cent of the computed normal tax. The surtax ranged from 17 per cent to a maximum of 85.5 per cent at the highest levels of taxable income. Taxes computed at various levels of taxable income are listed below:

| Taxable Income | Normal Tax | Surtax | Total Tax | Per Cent |
|---|---|---|---|---|
| 10,000 | 285 | 2,340 | 2,625 | 26.25 |
| 50,000 | 1,425 | 25,320 | 26,745 | 53.49 |
| 100,000 | 2,850 | 64,320 | 67,170 | 67.17 |
| 500,000 | 14,250 | 414,820 | 429,070 | 85.81 |
| 1,000,000 | 28,500 | 854,820 | 883,320 | 88.33 |
| above | | | + 86.45% | |

The 79th Congress also placed a limit on the taxes of any individual at 85.5 per cent. The withholding rate maximum was held at 19 per cent.

The 80th Congress on April 2, 1948 passed Public Law 80–471 HR 4790 An act "To reduce individual income tax payments, and for other purposes." The act was titled, "Revenue Act of 1948." Personal exemptions were increased from $500 to $600 and the Section 301 declared that the husband and wife joint return would use the same tax tables but would be required to pay 2 times the tax on one-half the taxable income on the joint return. Withholding maximum rate was set at 15 per cent. And the maximum tax was limited to 77 per cent of net income.

The tax reductions were as indicated in the table below:

| Computed Tax | Reduction |
|---|---|
| 0 to 400 | 17% |
| 400 to 100,000 | 68.00 +12% |
| over 100,000 | 12,020 + 9.75% |

The reductions in taxes collected were significant in line with the reduced expenditures as a result of the cessation of hostilities after World War II.

The 81st Congress on September 23, 1950 passed Public Law 81–814 HR 8920. An act "To provide Revenue, and for other purposes." The act was titled, "Revenue Act of 1950."

The tax reductions were further reduced—meaning there was a tax increase—as indicated below:

**1950 TAX REDUCTIONS**

| Computed Tax | Reduction |
|---|---|
| 0 to 400 | 13% |
| 400 to 100,000 | 52.00 +9% |
| over 100,000 | 9,016 + 7.3% |

Withholding was set at a maximum rate of 18 per cent, and the limitation on total taxes was set at 80 per cent of net income, but after September 30, 1950 the limitation was increased to 87 per cent.

For comparison purposes total taxes for various levels of taxable income are computed for 1948 and 1950 below:

| Taxable Income | Total Tax 1948 | Total Tax 1950 |
|---|---|---|
| 10,000 | 2,145 | 2,230 |
| 50,000 | 22,353 | 23,133 |
| 100,000 | 56,211 | 58,146 |
| 500,000 | 356,497 | 369,505 |
| 1,000,000 | 746,603 | 770,201 |

It was most unusual to pass a law that reduced the "reductions" to accomplish a true raise in taxes paid by all taxpayers. Perhaps the Congress wanted to impress the people by claiming that there really was some sort of "tax reduction" in the bill. Because that was the word used to describe the bill to the public—a bill to provide revenue and for other purposes. Over the years the Congress has been very reluctant to use the term "tax increase" even when there was a tax increase in the new tax bill.

The 82nd Congress Session I Chapter 521 passed HR 4473 on October 20, 1951, an act "To provide revenue, and for other purposes." The act was titled, "Revenue Act of 1951." The normal tax was set at 3 per cent and the surtax topped out at 88 per cent. Withholding was again increased to a rate of 20 per cent at the highest incomes. For comparison purposes the computed taxes are listed below:

| Taxable Income | Normal Tax | Surtax | Total Tax | Per Cent |
|---|---|---|---|---|
| 10,000 | 300 | 2,396 | 2,696 | 26.96 |
| 50,000 | 1,500 | 25,696 | 27,196 | 54.39 |
| 100,000 | 3,000 | 64,796 | 67,796 | 67.80 |
| 500,000 | 15,000 | 415,296 | 430,296 | 86.06 |
| 1,000,000 | 30,000 | 855,296 | 885,296 | 88.53 |
| above | | | + 91% | |

In 1954 the Congress made some sweeping changes to the Internal Revenue Code. The 83rd Congress 2nd Session passed HR 8300 an act "To revise the revenue laws of the United States." The act was titled, "Internal Revenue Code of 1954." While taxes were still held at a very high level for high income taxpayers, the significant change was in the treatment of long term capital gains. Capital gains were considered long term if the holding period was greater than six months, and there was introduced a 50 per cent deduction for all capital gains income. There was also provided an alternative capital gains rate of 25 per cent. Other provisions improved the investment climate for individuals by allowing a tax credit for dividends received by individuals.

In the debates over the bill, the minority view was that this law would provide income tax deductions to the investors, who at that time the minority claimed, only made up about 8 per cent of the population. Can you imagine a country as powerful as the United States, with only 8 per cent of the population investing in the future of their country? What a serious indictment of the existing tax policies, policies which motivated only 8 per cent of the people to have the courage to invest and take a risk to provide jobs, new technology, new products, improved productivity, real economic growth, and eventually more tax revenues to finance the Federal government. Computations of taxes at various levels of taxable income are listed below:

| Taxable Income | Total Tax | Per Cent |
|---|---|---|
| 10,000 | 2,640 | 26.40 |
| 50,000 | 26,820 | 53.64 |
| 100,000 | 67,320 | 67.32 |
| 500,000 | 429,820 | 85.96 |
| 1,000,000 | 884,820 | 88.48 |
| above | + 91% | |

Capital losses were limited to $1,000 and any excess could be carried over for five years.

**"What is most important for democracy is not that great fortunes should not exist, but that great fortunes should not remain in the same hands. In that way they do not form a class."** Alexis de Tocqueville.

The founding fathers of the United States propounded the principle that there should be a continuing circulation of the elite of the population from the citizenry into politics, from poor to rich, and back to their peaceful pursuits.

They never realized that there would eventually be "professional politicians" whose prime objective would be to be sure to get re-elected. Tocqueville could just as easily have stated that what is most important for democracy is that professional politicians should not exist, such political power should not remain in the same hands. In that way they would not form a class of persons who think only of getting reelected, forget the Federal Debt, forget continuing Federal Deficits, forget the loss of productivity, forget the lack of real growth in the economy, forget the loss of world markets, forget the terrible international trade balances. Get re-elected!

Minority (Democratic) Views stated in the history of legislation concerning the Internal Revenue Code of 1954, "This bill embodies a much-needed revision of the tax laws. ... To this extent, the bill is very commendable. Many substantive changes have been made, and in some instances these changes amount to a basic change in tax philosophy. Under the guise of removing obsolete language and inequitable provisions from present tax laws, the bill reduces taxes substantially for businesses, primarily corporations, and a few selected groups of individual taxpayers. This makes it much more than a simple reform of tax laws ... The average taxpayers that are benefited are literally few and far between, and the relief provided in these few scattered instances is negligible."

The minority showed their true colors when they stated, "We fully recognize that the process of investment is fundamental to our free enterprise system, but this does not mean that investment income should be given a tax advantage over other income ... Ninety two per cent of American families own no stock whatever. Of the remaining eight per cent, six-tenths of one per cent own 80 per cent of all publicly held stock. This means that the proposal of the majority would be reducing the taxes of only 8 per cent of American families, and primarily for the benefit of only six-tenths of 1 per cent."

The utter folly of the minority position is more clearly understood if one considers a set of tax laws that motivates only 8 per cent of the families to invest in the future of their country! Investment creates jobs, investment improves productivity, investment causes real economic growth, investment drives prices down for two reasons —investment is deferred consumption, so prices go down because of less demand, and investment creates more supply of goods, so prices go down because there is more supply of goods. The law of supply and demand is more fundamental than all the tax laws created in history.

What the country needed was more investment by more families, and the Tax Reform of 1954 provided the motivation to families to invest more and to become involved in the growing economy. The increased trend of personal investment continued to rise until the passage of the worst piece of tax legislation in the nation's history —The Tax Reform Act of 1969!

Further on the Minority views, the 1954 tax bill proposed first a $50 and then a $100 exclusion from income of dividends received by shareholders. The $50 exclusion would be provided in the first year of operation, and the $100 exclusion in the second and subsequent years. In addition a credit against tax would be provided for the remaining amount of dividends received by shareholders. In the first year of operation, this credit would be 5 per cent of the remaining dividends, and in the second and subsequent years would be 10 per cent in most cases.

The Minority stated that this provision would make a fundamental change in our tax philosophy, and it reflects more than any other provision in the bill the "trickle down" theory of taxation of the present administration. Certainly what the country needed was a change in tax philosophy if only 8 per cent of the families owned stocks. What was needed was a change in policy to motivate families to invest in the future of their country.

The Minority also stated that the proposal reverses the ability to pay principle of taxation and gives a tax advantage to unearned (investment) income over earned income from labor and services. They also stated, "We fully recognize that the process of investment is fundamental to our free-enterprise system, but this does not mean that investment income should be given a tax advantage over other income." It is interesting to find that the Minority did realize that investment is important, but they certainly did not realize that investment is not only important but actually is critical to the survival of a democracy. They did not realize that only 8 per cent of the nation's families investing is not sufficient to support the necessary requirements of real economic growth that must be attained if the country is to continue to grow its economy at a rate much greater than the growth rate of the population. There is no other way to improve a country's standard of living unless economic growth exceeds population growth.

Further Minority Views were that this is the wrong kind of tax relief at the wrong time, it is wrong in principle. "Adoption of this proposal would mean that those best able to pay their fair share of taxes would be given special tax treatment resulting in the shifting of the burden of taxation to those least able to bear it. We strenuously oppose this proposal."

The 1954 Tax law certainly did have a beneficial effect on the investment climate, since New York Stock Exchange data indicated that shareholders of public corporations as a per cent of U.S.

population grew from 4 per cent in 1950 to over 15 per cent by 1969. The 1969 Tax Reform Act did just the opposite, since it fouled up the investment climate so critically that the per cent of shareholders fell to 10 per cent by 1978. Such a lack of personal private investment caused high unemployment, high interest rates, high inflation, lower productivity growth, lower real economic growth, and horrible trends in our country's international trade balance. These are facts and not some empty economic theory. Tax policy does affect the personal private investment climate!

The tax law of 1954 was rather a long lasting bill that survived several years without change. Even the Public Law 37–834 HR 10650 passed an October 16, 1962 didn't change the rates of tax or the tax brackets. It was an Act, "To amend the Internal Revenue Code of 1954 to provide a credit for investment in certain depreciable property, to eliminate certain defects and inequities, and for other purposes" The bill was titled, "Revenue Act of 1962." The act provided a 7 per cent tax credit for investment in certain depreciable property used in the manufacture, production, extraction, transportation, communications, electrical energy, gas, water, or sewage disposal services, or a research or storage facility used in any of the above activities.

Facilities having a 4 year life would carry a 33.33 per cent of the tax credit, and those with a 6 year life would carry a 66.66 per cent of the tax credit, and any facility having a life greater than 8 years would carry the entire tax credit. The tax credit was limited to $50,000.

There were no meaningful changes in tax rates on individuals until the 88th Congress passed Public Law 88–272 HR8363 on February 26, 1964. It was an act, "To amend the Internal Revenue Code of 1954 to reduce individual and corporate income taxes, to make certain structural changes with respect to the income tax, and for other purposes." The bill was titled, "Revenue Act of 1964."

Taxes at various levels of taxable income are computed for 1964 and 1965 below:

| Taxable Income | 1964 Tax | Per Cent | 1965 Tax | Per Cent |
|---|---|---|---|---|
| 10,000 | 2,360 | 23.60 | 2,190 | 21.90 |
| 50,000 | 23,940 | 47.88 | 22,590 | 45.18 |
| 100,000 | 59,340 | 59.24 | 55,940 | 55.94 |
| 500,000 | 366,840 | 73.37 | 335,940 | 67.19 |
| 1,000,000 | 751,840 | 75.18 | 685,940 | 68.59 |
| | +77% | | + 70% | |

It can be seen that there truly were some reductions in taxes for all individuals. Section 201 reduced the tax credit for dividends received from 4 per cent to 2 per cent, but there was an off-setting increase in the exclusion of income from dividends received from $50 to $100. The maximum rate for withholding was set at 14 per cent. Capital gains were taxed at ordinary income tax rates on one-half the net long term capital gain.

Tax rates and other provisions were held for a period of three years before the Congress concluded that more revenue was needed to finance the ever growing expenditure levels. At the time public sentiment was growing in objection to the continually increasing Federal expenditures. By the end of 1965 Federal Debt had grown to 48 per cent of Gross Domestic Product and was at a level of $322.318 billion. The 1965 Federal Deficit was a mere $1.411 billion. The Congress was determined to take some steps toward reducing the deficit. The tax law of 1968 contained significant tax increases, but the battle to reduce expenditures was not won—by 1968 the deficit had grown to $25.161 billion, and the Federal Debt had reached $369.769 billion. The Congress at least tried to control Federal spending but it appeared to be a losing battle. The 1968 tax increases were very specific 7 per cent at all levels of taxable income.

The 90th Congress passed Public Law 90–364 HR 15414 on June 28, 1968. An act "To increase revenues, to limit expenditures and new obligational authority, and for other purposes." The bill was cited as, "Revenue and Expenditure Control Act of 1968."

The Congress tried to limit expenditures with this bill, but the record shows that there was no real restraint on spending. There was, however, a significant increase in all taxpayers' tax bills.

The bill imposed a surcharge of 7.5 per cent on each and every individuals' computed tax bills. to be reduced to only 5.0 per cent in the following year. The maximum withholding rate was increased to 33 per cent.

Section 201 provided that Federal employees be restricted to the number of employees as of June 30, 1966.

Section 202 provided for a reduction of 6 billion in expenditures during 1969.

Section 203 provided for a reduction in new obligational authority of 10 billion.

Section 204 required that the Administration submit recommendations for an 8 billion rescission in old obligational authority. The President to submit a report on recommendations to be included in his budget for fiscal year ending June 30, 1970.

There was a provision in the bill directing the President to study possible tax reforms to be submitted to the Congress.

The reforms contemplated in the tax bill of 1969 were purported to insure that all taxpayers pay their fair share of taxes. There also was a reduction in the top income tax rate from 70 per cent to 50 per cent for earned income. The top rate of tax on capital gains eventually reached 42.5 per cent. While everyone predicted that reducing ordinary income tax rates would be beneficial to the economy, the increase in capital gains tax rates more than over-powered the effects of the reduction in ordinary income tax rates. Ever since the passage of the Tax Reform Act of 1969, the economy has been in a steady decline.

Unemployment soared, inflation raged, productivity declined, interest rates rose to unheard-of levels, and Federal Deficits surged ahead, while Federal Debt continued to grow to unprecedented levels.

The Tax Reform Act of 1969 was the first in line to destroy the morality of the Internal Revenue Code, which over the years had hewn strictly to a high moral as well as legal code of procedure. That bill started a public outcry against the tax policies of our country, and that outcry is still being heard as proposals for a "flat tax" or other changes in the tax policies of our country to simplify and clarify the currently complex and complicated provisions of the

Internal Revenue Code are argued. Simplification is certainly needed, and changes to improve the personal, private investment climate are a vital necessity to start our country on a positive path to economic recovery and eventual economic security.

The start of the decline in the economic performance of the United States occurred after passage of the Tax Reform Act of 1969. A number of punitive provisions against private personal investors drove such investors to shun investment and to favor consumption. A number of provisions over-turned what had been a very moral and ethically sound Internal Revenue Code, and made it punitive and indeed anti-social to foundations, universities, and other charitable and educational institutions. As a result contributions and donations to charitable and educational institutions fell drastically.

The bill was Public Law 91–172 HR 13270 passed on December 30, 1969 An act "To reform the income tax laws." The act was titled, "Tax Reform Act of 1969." This act was supposedly to catch a few "rats" who were avoiding taxes, but the end result, as the economic performance over the last 26 years will prove, was that the law burned down the house to catch a few "rats."

One of the immoralities was the limitation on the deductibility of interest paid on loans made to increase an individual's investment. Another was the initiation of a "minimum tax" on tax preferences, which had been an important part of the laws up until 1969. The worst provision was the increase in the tax on capital gains from a maximum of 25 per cent to 42.5 per cent. There was also an addition to all taxes in 1970 with the surcharge of 2.5 per cent added to all taxes computed in 1970.

For comparison purposes taxes at various levels of taxable income are computed for both 1969 and 1970:

| Taxable Income | Total Tax 1969 | Total Tax 1970 |
|---|---|---|
| 10,000 | 1,820 | 1,865.50 |
| 50,000 | 15,020 | 15,395.50 |
| 100,000 | 37,980 | 38,929.50 |
| 500,000 | 320,980 | 329,004.50 |
| 1,000,000 | 670,980 | 687,754.50 |
| | + 70% | + 71.75% |

For wage earners and salaried individuals the maximum tax rate was held at 50 per cent in 1969 and 51.25 per cent in 1970.

The act created a minimum tax on all sorts of tax preferences whenever such tax preference exceeded $30,000. The minimum tax started at 10 per cent in 1969. Later tax bills increased the rate to much higher levels.

Observing the economic performance of the United States after the passage of this horrible tax reform act shows a country that once was the economic leader of the world enduring continuing Federal Deficits and sliding deeper and deeper into debt as the years went by.

The plunge in Real Economic Growth, the rise in unemployment, the loss in productivity growth, the rise in inflation, and the soaring interest rates all made life much more difficult for the citizens of the United States. Even the price-earnings ratios of listed shares plunged from a level of 16 to as low as 6, forcing corporations to flock to the debt markets to raise vitally needed capital to carry out their business plans. The evidence is clear—reducing ordinary income tax rates, while increasing the tax on capital gains, and adding the complexity and complications of "minimum taxes" making investment decisions much more difficult for individuals—lack of investment by individuals leads to a deteriorating economy.

The 91st Congress passed HR 13270 on December 30, 1969, and created the worst environment for individual investors in the nation's history. In addition private foundations were directly attacked, and contributions to charitable and educational institutions were made much more difficult. The nation's tax laws which had been based on sound moral principles, were changed to veer from those principles. The effect on the nation's economy was devastating. In the next six years the following economic changes took place:

1. Annual growth in Real Gross National Product fell from an average of 4.335 per cent per year in the nine years prior to 1969 to an average of 1.657 per cent per year in the six years after 1969.
2. Annual Productivity Increases fell from an average of 3.23 per cent per year in the nine years prior to 1969 to an average of 1.529 per cent per years in the six years after 1969.

3. Annual U.S. Merchandise Trade Balance fell from a positive 40 billion in 1969 to 30 billion by 1974.
4. Federal budget surplus of over 3 billion in 1969 was followed by continuing deficits reaching 75 billion by 1976.
5. Federal Debt rose to $650 billion by 1976.

The "Tax Reform Act of 1969" started the decline of the United States as the world's most powerful country. Real economic growth declined, Federal Deficits soared, productivity declined, and the Merchandise trade balance fell from a positive 40 billion to negative 100 billion over the following years.

Provisions of the law raised the capital gains tax to as high as 42.5 per cent, the tax surcharge was held at 10 per cent for 1969 and was reduced to 2.5 per cent in 1970. The provisions that deteriorated the personal private investment climate were the increase in the capital gains tax, the 50 per cent write-off of capital losses, and the restriction on the deductibility of interest paid on money borrowed for investment purposes. Those three provisions were clear to all investors, the message from the Congress was, "don't invest, don't invest, don't invest." And individuals did curtail their investments. For example, in 1969 there were 80.7 million in the labor force with 30.8 million investors, by 1975 the labor force had grown to 93 million, but investors had shrunk to 25.27 million. If investors had invested at the same rate in 1975 as they had in 1969, there would have been 35.5 million investors. By 1975 the average portfolio of each investor was $10,100. With investors at the same percentage of the work force an additional 103 billion of equity capital would have been available to provide new jobs, and new services. The lack of investment had caused the unemployment rate to rise to nearly 10 per cent of the work force. The 103 billion of equity capital could have created over 4 million new jobs and would have reduced the unemployment rate to just over 3 per cent!

The tragedy was that 1800 companies went to the equity markets for new capital in 1969 and by 1975, only 150 were able to raise new capital. The further tragedy was that small companies with net worth of 5 million or less raised over 1.1 billion of new capital in 1969, but by 1974 those kinds of companies raised only 10 million in new equity capital.

Department of Commerce data indicated that these small companies create new jobs at a rate over 60 times that of large companies. Up to that time the Tax Reform Act of 1969 was the worst piece of legislation ever foisted on the American public. The country has been in financial trouble ever since.

The 94th Congress 2nd Session passed HR 10612 on October 4, 1976. An act "To reform the tax laws of the United States." The bill was titled, "Tax Reform Act of 1976."

With its signing by President Ford, the Tax Reform Act of 1976 became part of the law of the land. The act was several years in development and represented the most extensive and far-reaching piece of tax legislation since the enactment of the 1954 Code. The total package was hardly a model of tax legislation. The Wall Street Journal castigated the bill as rivaling "Tolstoi in complexity and Dostoevski in gloom."

The reform provisions continue the trend of recent years to make it more difficult for wealthier taxpayers to avoid taxes by taking advantage of various incentive provisions of the law. Toward this end, the minimum tax has been toughened and increased. Deductions for tax shelters have been limited. The holding period for capital gains has been lengthened. Numerous other provisions will have the effect of increasing taxes. The holding period for capital gains was lengthened to nine months for 1977 and to one year for 1978 and after. And capital losses were limited to $2,000.00 per individual.

Taxes at various levels of taxable income are listed below:

**MARRIED FILING JOINT RETURN**

| Taxable Income | Total Tax | Per Cent |
|---|---|---|
| 10,000 | 1,152 | 11.52 |
| 50,000 | 15,460 | 30.92 |
| 100,000 | 43,260 | 43.26 |
| 500,000 | 318,740 | 63.54 |
| 1,000,000 | 668,740 | 66.87 |
| | + 70% | |

**SINGLE INDIVIDUALS**

| Taxable Income | Total Tax | Per Cent |
|---|---|---|
| 10,000 | 1,542 | 15.42 |
| 50,000 | 18,870 | 37.54 |
| 100,000 | 51,572 | 51.57 |
| 500,000 | 331,550 | 66.31 |
| 1,000,000 | 681,550 | 68.16 |

Capital losses after December 31, 1977 were to be limited to $3,000. The 50 per cent deduction for capital gains was retained but the alternative capital gains tax, if applicable was limited to a gain of no more than $50,000. One-half of the Capital gain was an item of tax preference subject to a tax at 15 per cent.

Section 163(d) limited the amount of investment interest that could be deducted to $10,000 plus any investment income.

There were also personal exemptions of $750 per individual, and there was a tax credit of $35 per person, and a $3,200 deduction for married persons filing a joint return to arrive at a tax credit that if an individual's income was large enough was limited to $180. Even more complications for a bedraggled taxpayer!

Complexity and complication was the order of the day in all tax legislation since 1969. Simplicity and morality was the order of the day in Ways and Means and Senate Finance in the years prior to 1969.

## *The Tax Law of 1977*

Public Law 95–30 HR 3477 passed on May 23, 1977 was an act, "To reduce individual and business income taxes and to provide tax simplification and reform." The law was to be titled, "The Tax Reduction and Simplification Act of 1977."

There were no significant changes in the law but there were some slight tax reductions:

| Taxable Income | Married | Single |
|---|---|---|
| 10,000 | 1,152 | 1,342 |
| 50,000 | 15,460 | 18,870 |
| 100,000 | 43,260 | 51,572 |
| 500,000 | 318,740 | 331,550 |
| 1,000,000 | 668,740 | 681,550 |

The next year some of the effects of the author's campaign to reduce taxes on long term capital gains were incorporated into the law. While there were some slight reductions in taxes at all levels, the significant change was in the treatment of long term capital gains.

## *The Tax Law of 1978*

Public Law 95–600 HR 13511 passed on November 6, 1978. It was as act "To amend the Internal Revenue Code of 1954 to reduce income taxes, and for other purposes."

| Taxable Income | Married | Single |
|---|---|---|
| 10,000 | 1,062 | 1,387 |
| 50,000 | 14,778 | 18,067 |
| 100,000 | 41,998 | 50,053 |
| 500,000 | 316,724 | 329,887 |
| 1,000,000 | 666,724 | 679,887 |

The personal exemption was raised to $1,000 and a 60 per cent deduction was instituted for all long term capital gains. That provision resulted in the tax rate for long term capital gains ranging from 5.6 per cent at the lowest levels to 20 to 28 per cent at the highest levels. Such a provision motivated individuals to invest more in the subsequent years than had been the practice in the years prior to 1978. The resurgence in investment was evident almost immediately as the number of shareholders of New York Stock Exchange shares increased appreciably in the next few years.

The alternative minimum tax was changed to 10 per cent for alternative tax incomes between 20,000 and 60,000 and to 20 per cent for ATI between 60,000 and 100,000, and to 25 per cent for ATI over 100,000.

The Congress was still worried about the lack of real economic growth and debated long and hard about the tax policies that would nurture such growth. It appears that the Congress was still not aware of the detrimental effects of tax policy upon individual's decisions either to invest or to consume, and in turn its longer term effect upon the real economic growth of the country.

Personal savings and personal investment are essential to the continued development of the country in economic power, diplomatic power, and the well-being of its citizens, and ultimately its standard of living. While education and technology are necessary ingredients to real economic growth, without capital investment, no country can grow and improve its productivity and ultimate standard of living.

In a marathon weekend session before adjournment, the 95th Congress approved major tax legislation, including the Revenue Act of 1978. The revenue act is a comprehensive tax package providing, among other things, an $18.7 billion tax cut for individuals and businesses. The act was signed by the President on November 6, 1978, as Public Law 95–600.

The act established five categories of tax rates:

1. Married Individuals Filing Joint Returns
2. Married Individuals Filing Separate Returns
3. Single Individuals
4. Head of a Household
5. Estates and Trusts

For comparison purposes, computations of taxes at various income levels are listed below for categories 1 and 3:

**CATEGORY 1**

| Taxable Income | Total Tax | Rate on Excess Income | Per Cent |
|---|---|---|---|
| 10,000 | 1,062 | 18% | 10.62 |
| 50,000 | 14,778 | 49% | 29.56 |
| 100,000 | 47,902 | 59% | 47.90 |
| 500,000 | 316,724 | 70% | 63.34 |
| 1,000,000 | 666,724 | 70% | 66.67 |

**CATEGORY 3**

| Taxable Income | Total Tax | Rate on Excess Income | Per Cent |
|---|---|---|---|
| 10,000 | 1,387 | 21% | 13.87 |
| 50,000 | 18,067 | 55% | 36.13 |
| 100,000 | 50,053 | 68% | 50.05 |
| 500,000 | 329,887 | 70% | 65.97 |
| 1,000,000 | 679,887 | 70% | 67.99 |

The important change in treatment of capital gains improved the investment climate in the country. For capital gains realized after October, 1978, non-corporate taxpayers may deduct 60 per cent of any net capital gain. That provision reduced the capital gains rate of tax to 5.6 per cent at the lowest levels of income and to 28 per cent at the highest levels.

The act retained some of the minimum tax complexities, which still clouded investment decisions. For instance the act provided that the capital gains deduction was not to be taken into account for the 15 per cent add-on minimum tax but was to be subject to the new alternative minimum tax. The Congress added some more confusing aspects of the Internal Revenue Code. The maximum tax rate on earned income was preserved at a level of 50 per cent. There was a catch, however, since the amount of personal service income eligible for the maximum tax must be reduced dollar for dollar by the amount of the taxpayers tax preferences for the taxable year, including capital gains. But the 1978 law eliminates the capital gains preference item as a reduction in personal service income. How's that for more complexity in the tax law?

Imagine having to worry about the add-on minimum tax and also the alternative minimum tax and how they interact, when trying to make an important or even critical investment decision.

Personal exemptions were increased from $750 to $1,000, and additional exemptions were provided for taxpayers over 65 years of age and further exemptions were provided for blind taxpayers. The earned income credit for lower level taxpayers was more complex, since it was phased out for earned incomes above $5,000, but amounted to 10 per cent of the first $5,000 and was reduced by 12.5 per cent of any income in excess of $6,000. Further complications!

## *1985 Office of Tax Analysis Report*

A specific report to the Congress on the "Capital Gains Tax Reductions of 1978"[3] was published in September of 1985. In an overview the report stated that the 1978 Revenue Act reduced the taxation of capital gains. The specific changes were:

1. The reduction of the fraction of net long term capital gains included in taxable income from 50 per cent to 40 per cent.
2. The elimination of the untaxed portion of capital gains from the list of tax preferences subject to an add-on minimum tax.
3. The elimination of the "poisoning" of the maximum tax on personal service income by the untaxed portion of capital gains.
4. The reduction in the tax rate on corporate capital gains from 30 per cent to 28 per cent.

A further provision set the maximum marginal tax rate of 25 per cent on net long term capital gains as an alternative tax. (The "Economic Recovery Act of 1981" further reduced the maximum tax rate on net long term capital gains to 20 per cent.)

The report concluded that over time the capital gains tax reductions resulted in a higher rate of investment, higher capital stock, higher national income, higher labor productivity, and higher overall standard of living than if such reductions had not been enacted. All income groups benefited due to the increases in capital stock and labor productivity.

The 1978 Act resulted in substantial unlocking of investments, and increased capital gains realizations. The report's cross-section approach predicted an increase in realizations sufficiently large to result in a large long run increase in federal revenue.

The report concluded that the 1978 law changes in capital gains tax rates reduced the "lock-in effect." The movement of capital from tax-favored industries to other private sector activities increases the average productivity of the capital stock, raising national income and economic welfare. Reduced taxation of capital gains is likely to increase the supply of funds available to venture capital firms from high income individuals. ... reduced taxation of capital gains is likely to encourage entrepreneurs to establish new enterprises and thus expand the opportunities available to venture capitalists. (A Labor Department Report indicated that small firms created new jobs at a rate Over 60 times greater than large industries.)

The 1985 report did not study the effects upon employment, although it concluded that labor productivity was improved by the increased capital stock stimulated by the reductions in the capital gains tax. If capital was flowing to entrepreneurs and venture capitalists, the Labor Department Report would indicate that there was a significant increase in the number of jobs created after the 1978 Tax Act.

The Report concluded that "any effort to raise substantial revenue by increasing capital gains tax rates, given the current parameters of the tax law, is likely to be ineffective.

The interesting criticism of the report is that no study was made of the consequences of raising capital gains tax rates, that did occur in the "Tax Reform Act of 1969" and later the "Revenue Act of 1976." Over those six years inflation skyrocketed to 13 per cent, interest rates climbed to 15 per cent, unemployment rose to 10 per cent, growth of real gross national product dropped from 4.335 per cent per year to 1.657 per cent averaged over the next six years, annual productivity growth dropped from 3.23 per cent to 1.529 per cent averaged over those same six years.

The report did conclude that no significant increase in the savings rate of the nation was observed, since a significant portion of the returns on savings is in the form of dividends, interest, and rental income.

The report also didn't address the serious balance of trade swings from a positive trade balance growth of 4 Billion per year for the nine years prior to 1969, to a negative growth of 1.15 Billion per year after the 1969 Tax Law was passed. The United States International Trade Balance has become one of the country's most serious economic problems. Such swings in international trade are the result of lack of productivity growth over the years, because of the lack of high levels of capital investment. Over the years Japan has invested over twice as much in their economy as the United States, and that has allowed their productivity to increase tremendously, especially with respect to that of the United States.

## *The Tax Law of 1981*

Public Law 97–34 HR 4242 was passed on August 13, 1981, it was an Act "To amend the Internal Revenue Code of 1954 to encourage economic growth through the reduction of tax rates for individual taxpayers, acceleration of capital cost recovery of investments in plant, equipment, and real property, and incentives for savings, and for other purposes." It was to be titled, "Economic Recovery Act of 1981."

The act provided for reductions in taxes for all individuals over the next three years, and it is important to show the different tax levels for married taxpayers filing joint returns and for single taxpayers:

**MARRIED TAXPAYERS FILING JOINT RETURNS**

| Taxable Income | 1982 Tax | 1983 Tax | 1984 Tax |
|---|---|---|---|
| 10,000 | 930 | 864 | 819 |
| 50,000 | 13,305 | 12,014 | 11,368 |
| 100,000 | 34,190 | 34,190 | 32,400 |
| 500,000 | 237,449 | 234,002 | 231,400 |
| 1,000,000 | 487,449 | 484,002 | 481,400 |
| **SINGLE TAXPAYERS FILING SEPARATE RETURNS** | | | |
| 10,000 | 1,233 | 1,121 | 1,075 |
| 50,000 | 16,318 | 14,738 | 13,385 |
| 100,000 | 41,318 | 39,473 | 37,935 |
| 500,000 | 214,318 | 239,473 | 237,935 |
| 1,000,000 | 491,318 | 489,473 | 487,935 |

One can see that the tax reductions were rather minuscule over the three years, but the significant change was the reduction in the tax on long term capital gains. There was a 20 per cent maximum tax on long term capital gains and also a 60 per cent deduction on any long term capital gain. Such provisions made the tax on capital gains range from a low of 4.8 per cent to a maximum of 20 per cent. There were also some savings provisions such as a $2,000 exemption for certain types of savings.

These provisions motivated individuals to invest and save more than at any time since the terrible tax law of 1969. The country started to respond to such positive provisions, and economic growth started to improve.

While the tax law of 1981 made no significant changes to the tax rates, certain changes in the alternative minimum tax provisions did add a measure of complexity in the tax laws that made investments more difficult to make. The alternative minimum tax rate was installed at 20 per cent of any alternative minimum taxable income. And that complexity was certainly not good tax policy to motivate individuals to invest rather than consume. Complexity in our tax laws is detrimental to individuals in their pursuit of their long term objectives, and yet does very little to increase the total tax revenues of our nation. The entire concept of alternative minimum taxes is adding complexity with very little improvement in the total revenues collected. The way to increase revenues is to create real economic growth. Such real economic growth can only come from more personal, private investment. The study of the economy of Great Britain over 100 years proves that.

## *The Tax Law of 1984*

Public Law 98–369 HR 4170 passed or July 18, 1984 as an act, "To provide for tax reform and for deficit reduction." The act was titled, "The Deficit Reduction Act of 1984."

There were no significant changes to the tax rates and it was difficult to see any changes that would truly reduce Federal Deficits. The law appeared to be a palliative to constituents back home, so that the Congressmen and Senators could say we really tried to get some reduction in the Federal Deficit. The Federal Deficit actually increased from $185.388 billion in 1984 to $212.334 billion in 1985.

Try as they might the legislators had no control over the budget or the deficit and the Federal Debt climbed from $1.564 trillion in 1984 to $1.817 trillion in 1985. What a terrible performance by legislators leading the public to believe that they were really concerned about the Federal Deficits. Obviously they were more interested in being sure that they were reelected than providing proper legislation to insure that such deficits and further borrowing should not be tolerated. Certainly they were the "many that didn't care!" That performance was another reason for your author deciding to write.

## *The Tax Law of 1985*

Public Law 94–44 The T&E Law was supposedly passed to simplify matters for taxpayers. What happened was almost exactly the opposite: the new 1985 laws introduced still more complications to an already complex system with new rules for 1985, 1986, and future years. There were fifteen or sixteen brackets with tax rates ranging from 11 per cent at the lowest levels of income and 50 per cent at the highest levels: over 175,250 for married and over 88,270 for single. Tax levels for 1986 are presented below:

| Taxable Income | Married | Single |
|---|---|---|
| 10,000 | 772.90 | 1,025.40 |
| 50,000 | 6,959.90 | 13,117.80 |
| 100,000 | 31,403.00 | 36,981.00 |
| 500,000 | 229,928.50 | 236,981.00 |
| 1,000,000 | 475,928.50 | 486,981.00 |

The personal exemption was increased from $1,000 to $1,080 and record keeping requirements were significantly more complicated.

Certainly the effects of the "Deficit Reduction Act of 1984" were not apparent since the total deficit for 1986 increased from $212.334 billion in 1985 to $221.245 billion. Even two years after the passage of that phony bill there were no reductions in the Federal

Deficit. The total irresponsibility of the House and Senate is still manifest in the terrible financial performance of the country. The results of these do-nothing laws led the author to conclude that "Nobody Cares." Later research revealed that some really did care and their proposals for improvement are elicited later in the book. The tax law of 1986 was the last straw for the author, since some of the provisions of that law were extremely detrimental to our country's financial performance with deficits rising to over $290 billion by 1992. More tax law history to come.

The 99th Congress on October 22, 1986 passed HR 3838 Public Law 99–514, an act "To reform the tax laws of the United States." It was titled the "Tax Reform Act of 1986."

The President Ronald Reagan was led to believe that this law was a real improvement in the tax legislation, because of its simplicity. The President was told that the personal exemptions for 1987, 1988, and 1989 were increased to $1,900, $1,950, and $2,000 respectively. He was also told that the law was significantly simplified by having only two brackets for individual tax computations: personal taxes were 15 per cent for all incomes up to 29,750, and 28 per cent for all incomes over 29,750. President Reagan probably considered this bill to be a true simplification of the tax laws. No one told him that the rates were significantly changed for 1987:

| Taxable Income | Total Tax | Per Cent |
|---|---|---|
| 10,000 | 1,380 | 13.80 |
| 50,000 | 10,590 | 21.18 |
| 100,000 | 28,800 | 28.80 |
| 500,000 | 182,800 | 36.56 |
| 1,000,000 | 375,300 | 37.53 |
| above | + 38.5% | |

The alternative Minimum tax rate was increased to 21 per cent. The deduction for capital gains of 60 per cent was eliminated and a maximum rate of 28 per cent was substituted as the rate for capital gains. The capital loss allowance was set at $3,000. The individual dividends received exclusion was repealed, making it even more difficult for individual investors.

The 60 per cent deduction for capital gains was repealed, and since it no longer was a part of the law, it is no longer a tax preference. The horrible result, not anticipated by the Congress was that the tax rate on long term capital gains was increased as much as 648 per cent on lower level income taxpayers, and for taxpayers in the intermediate range of income at $20,000 the capital gains tax rate was increased as much as 125 per cent. Certainly no thinking Senator or Congressman would have voted for such a change in the tax laws if they had been told by their consulting economists and advisors that such a result would be produced by the tax law of 1986!

If the Tax Reform law of 1969 was bad for the economy, the 1986 tax law was at least as bad or perhaps even worse than the tax law of 1969. Senator Alan Cranston in his remarks before the Senate strongly pointed out that what the Senate Finance committee was considering—the repeal of the 60 per cent deduction for capital gains—was in his words, "total economic insanity." Senator Cranston was right, because the economic performance of the country in the last nine years bears out his claim—continually increasing Federal Debt and no program of any kind to pay off the debt or even to balance the Federal budget. The total financial irresponsibility of the House and the Senate is reprehensible, and must not be condoned. The future of our country is in dire jeopardy with the ever increasing Federal debt, and with no conscious program for taking the steps to reverse the serious trends in continuing Federal Deficits. Powerful nations have fallen in the past because of the total financial irresponsibility of their government leaders. Over and over again we have shown that significant improvements in our country's personal, private investment climate can help to solve our country's serious problems of continuing Federal Deficits and ever growing Federal debt.

## *A Study of the Flow of Individual Income Taxes*

In 1934 individual income taxes paid amounted to $420 million out of $2.955 billion in total Federal Receipts, which represents 14.2 per cent of all revenues. In only five years individual income taxes grew at a rate of 19.6 per cent per year to a level of $1.029 billion. By that time such taxes represented 16.3 per cent of total Federal Revenues of $6.295 billion.

The requirements to finance the ever-growing expenditures of World War II, forced the collection of individual income taxes to shoot up at a rate of 83.1 per cent per year to a level of $19.705 billion which amounted to over 45 per cent of all Federal Revenues. Even with the accelerating collection of taxes, the Federal Deficit reached $48.735 billion at the end of 1944, and the Federal Debt amounted to $204.079 billion or about 101 per cent of the nation's Gross National Product.

At the end of hostilities in 1945, it would seem logical that Federal requirements for funding the expenditures during the war would fall significantly. It is interesting to note the flow of individual income taxes in the years following 1944:

| Year | INDIVIDUAL INCOME TAXES |
|---|---|
| 1945 | 18,372,000,000 |
| 1946 | 16,098,000,000 |
| 1947 | 17,935,000,000 |
| 1948 | 19,315,000,000 |
| 1949 | 15,552,000,000 |
| 1950 | 15,775,000,000 |
| 1951 | 21,616,000,000 |

After 1951 there were only a few years where a reduction in taxes was experienced by individuals:

| Year | INDIVIDUAL INCOME TAXES |
|---|---|
| 1952 | 27,934,000,000 |
| 1953 | 29,816,000,000 |
| 1954 | 29,542,000,000* |
| 1955 | 28,747,000,000* |
| 1956 | 32,188,000,000 |
| 1957 | 35,620,000,000 |
| 1958 | 34,724,000,000* |
| 1959 | 36,719,000,000 |

Individual income taxes continued to grow consistently for the next eleven years to $90.412 billion in 1970. There was a decrease to $86.23 billion in 1971, but, after that year, taxes continued to grow until they reached $297.744 billion in 1982. In 1983 taxes dropped to $288.938 billion, but since that time taxes have increased each year eventually exceeding $500 billion per year.

With such increases in tax revenues it would seem possible to create surpluses each year and eventually reduce the Federal Debt. In the sixty-one years since 1934 there have only been eight years where the country has been able to experience surpluses. In 1947, 1948, and 1949 surpluses of $4.018 billion, 11.796 billion, and 580 million were generated. In 1951 the surplus was $6.102 billion. In 1956 and 1957 surpluses of $3.947 billion and $3.412 billion were experienced. In 1960 the surplus reached $301 million and in 1969, the last year of any surplus, the level was $3.242 billion.

Since 1969 each year has shown deficit after deficit and the Federal Debt has grown from $50.696 billion to over $5 trillion.

The famous Hudson Institute conducted a meeting in Los Angeles in 1977 and raised a question about the lessons to be learned from history. History had shown that whenever there was a war or hostilities of some kind, prices always rose precipitously during the war. After the war prices always retreated to their pre-war levels. Such was true after the Revolutionary War, after the War of 1812, the Civil War, the Spanish American War, and World War I. After World War II prices remained relatively high. Hudson Institute people asked the audience, "Why is this price experience after World War II so different from prior history?"

The author was in the audience, and suggested the following:

"After each war all citizens were aware of the taxes that were being levied upon them, and as soon as hostilities were over, those citizens reacted to continuing high taxes, and put pressure on their legislators to reduce taxes and spending. The reduced spending allowed prices to fall to the pre-war levels. After World War II, citizens were not aware of the severe tax load on them, because of one piece of legislation—Withholding of taxes. Citizens had no feeling for the taxes being collected because they did not have to raise the money after the end of each year to pay the taxes in one lump sum. In fact most people were happy to receive a refund of over-withheld taxes and were very happy to have such a nice "dividend."

There was no pressure on the legislators to reduce taxes because most citizens never saw or held the money that was quietly taken from them in such a painless way. From the legislator's point of view, money was flowing into the Treasury at such a fast and regular rate that spending was no problem. Spending continued to grow, and with the spending growth there was no possibility to have prices recede to pre-war levels.

The real culprit here was the most insidious tax law of all, "The Current Tax Payment Act of 1943," where money was taken from taxpayers without their ever seeing it or holding it. The method was painless. The palliative was the "dividend" to taxpayers that came from over-withholding of taxes at the source. That led to a high percentage of taxpayers that "didn't care" about taxes. Hopefully, taxpayers are beginning to care, and if they make their concerns known, it is possible to make the changes to get our country moving in the right direction again.

While the Tax Reform Act of 1969 was the first serious attack on the investment climate in the United States, and the 1976 changes further attacked the then critically poor investment climate even further, changes in 1978 and 1980 started to improve the climate for personal private investment. The 1986 Tax Reform Act had many good provisions regarding many "Tax Shelters" and other non-productive investments, however, the treatment of long term capital gains bordered on being unbelievably horrible. Imagine the effects on smaller investors:

Investors with no other income, but a $20,000 net long term capital gain had their taxes increased 648 per cent! If another investor had $20,000 in other income and a $20,000 net long-term capital gain his taxes would increase 125 per cent! How many millions of people in such a range of income and capital gains were affected by such provisions of tax reform can only be estimated but it is a large number.

The serious loser was the entire country. Less private personal investment resulted in less improvement in productivity, less real economic growth, fewer jobs, less tax revenues, and with continually increasing Federal spending, ever-increasing Federal Debt.

But as usual no one in Congress seemed to care. In 1986 the Federal Debt had reached 2.13 Trillion and was projected to grow to almost 2.6 Trillion by 1988. No one seemed to care even though the interest payments to service that debt had increased to 117.9 Billion, in 1986.

One simple change in the law would have overcome all the difficulties created by the 1986 treatment of long term capital gains. The re-enactment of Section 1202(a) the 60 per cent deduction for long term capital gains, and Section 1222(3) the six-month holding period. Such an improvement would lower the effective rates of tax on long term capital gains to between 11.2 and 13.2 per cent. Such a range of rates would maximize total capital gains taxes paid. Lower rates result in more revenues. Studies have proven this over the years.

While the Tax Reform Act of 1986 purported to simplify the tax laws, the law was actually much more complex and complicated than previous laws. Supposedly there were only two rates of tax, 15 per cent and 28 per cent, but that really wasn't true. For that tax year the rates were actually 15 per cent and 28 per cent but there was a 5 per cent surtax at the highest levels of income. For comparison purposes the computed taxes at various levels of taxable income are listed below for married filing a joint return and for single individuals:

| Taxable Income | Total Tax | Per Cent |
|---|---|---|
| 10,000 | 1,500.00 | 15.00 |
| 50,000 | 10,132.50 | 20.26 |
| 100,000 | 25,537.50 | 25.54 |
| 500,000 | 157,519.50 | 31.50 |
| 1,000,000 | 322,537.50 | 32.25 |
| | | |
| 10,000 | 1,500 | 15.00 |
| 50,000 | 12,022 | 24.04 |
| 100,000 | 28,522 | 28.52 |
| 500,000 | 160,522 | 32.10 |
| 1,000,000 | 325,522 | 32.55 |

There were further phasing out of personal and dependency exemptions that complicated the computation of taxes, and were really disguised tax increases.

The personal exemptions for a husband and wife filing a joint return amounted to $1,900 for 1987, $1,950 for 1988, and $2,000 in 1989. The personal exemptions were phased out for higher income taxpayers, for married filing jointly as income exceeded $149,250 the exemption was phased out, such that for each additional income of $10,920 a total exemption was phased out. For single taxpayers the phase-out started at an income level of $89,560. What a tricky way to tax higher paid taxpayers at much higher rates than those publicly advertised as tax reduction rates.

One positive provision changed the capital loss treatment from deducting only 50 per cent of any long term loss, to full deduction of any long term capital loss, but limited the deductible loss to $3,000 against ordinary income each year.

Another interesting provision of the tax law made it necessary to include a portion of Social Security benefits as income if married taxpayers had base income over $32,000 and single taxpayers had a base income over $25,000. The theory was that since employers had contributed one-half of all contributions to your Social Security account, higher level taxpayers could afford to pay income tax on the half of Social Security benefits received. Another way to increase taxes on the higher income taxpayers. Subtle but effective in adding a tax load to higher paid taxpayers, without "raising taxes."

Income averaging which allowed a taxpayer to spread his income over a four year period was repealed for tax years after 1986. The alternative minimum tax rate was set at 21 per cent, and again complicated the tax laws to make critical investment decisions ever more difficult. Even the $40,000 exemption for the alternative minimum tax phased out for higher level taxpayers, phasing out at 25 cents per dollar for every dollar that alternative minimum taxable income exceeds $150,000 for married person filing jointly, and for single persons having income above $112,500. Certainly the Congress made it much more difficult for high level income taxpayers.

The 100th Congress Session I on December 22, 1987 passed Public Law 100–203 HR 3545, an Act "To provide reconciliation pursuant to section 4 of the concurrent resolution on the budget for the fiscal year 1988." The act was titled, "Omnibus Budget Reconciliation Act of 1987." There were no meaningful changes in the rates of tax, but certain actions were taken to create a National Economic Commission under Title II of the act.section 201.

The National Economic Commission shall make specific recommendations regarding the following:

1. Methods to reduce the Federal budget deficit while promoting economic growth and encouraging saving and capital formation.
2. A means of ensuring that the burden of achieving the Federal budget deficit reduction goals does not undermine economic growth and is equitably distributed and not borne disproportionately by any one economic group, social group, region or State.

The Commission shall report to the President by March 1, 1989 recommendations voted by a majority of Commission members. The Commission to hold hearings, obtain assistance from Federal Agencies Staff pay not to exceed GS–18, and expenses to be limited to $1,000,000. The Commission will be subject to audit by the Controller General. The Commission ceases to exist 30 days after submittal of the report.

It appears that the Commission was not very successful in arriving at any meaningful recommendations, since no progress has been made in reducing Federal budget deficits in the years that followed.

The 101st Congress passed Public Law 101–508 HR 5835 on November 5, 1990. An act "To provide for reconciliation pursuant to section 4 of the concurrent resolution on the budget for fiscal year 1991." The act was titled "Omnibus Budget Reconciliation Act of 1990." Title IX Revenue Provisions Section 11001 was titled "Revenue Reconciliation Act of 1990."

There were some changes in the rates of tax at all levels of income and the computed taxes at various levels of taxable income are listed below:

| Taxable Income | Joint Return Taxes | | Single Return Taxes | |
|---|---|---|---|---|
| 10,000 | 1,500.00 | 15.00% | 1,500 | 15.00% |
| 50,000 | 9,781.50 | 19.56% | 11,560 | 23.12% |
| 100,000 | 24,429.50 | 24.43% | 27,060 | 27.06% |
| 500,000 | 148,429.50 | 29.68% | 151,060 | 30.20% |
| 1,000,000 | 303,429.50 | 30.34% | 306,060 | 30.61% |
| above | + 31% | | + 31% | |

The maximum capital gains rate was 28 per cent. And higher level taxpayers had a further tax increase, since the personal exemptions were phased out for married individuals at an income level of $150,000 with a 2 per cent reduction in the personal exemption for each $2,500 of income over the threshold level, and for single taxpayers the threshold level was $100,000. There were further complications involving itemized deductions for taxpayers with incomes over $100,000. Itemized deductions were limited to the lesser of 3 per cent of every dollar of income over $100,000, or with incomes over $100,000 limited to 80 per cent of the itemized deductions. A very sneaky way to tax higher level income taxpayers at higher than the published rates of tax! And the alternative minimum tax rate was increased from 21 to 24 per cent.

The 103rd Congress passed Public Law 103–66 HE 2264 on August 10, 1993. An act "To provide for reconciliation pursuant to section 7 of the concurrent resolution on the budget for fiscal year 1994." The act was titled, "Omnibus Budget Reconciliation Act of 1993."

Title XIII Chapter 1 Revenue Provisions was titled, "Revenue Reconciliation Act of 1993." Section 1202 provided for a 50 per cent exclusion from gain from certain small business stock. Section 1202 (k) (b) Required one-half the exclusion to be treated as a preference for minimum tax purposes. (The Congress giveth and the Congress taketh away!) Section 1044 provided for the rollover of gain from sale of Publicly Traded Securities into Specialized Small Business Investment Companies. There was a limitation on the amount of gains rolled over to $50,000.

There were also some tax rate increases and the computations are listed below:

| Taxable Income | Joint Return Taxes | | Single Return Taxes | |
|---|---|---|---|---|
| 10,000 | 1,500.00 | 15.00% | 1,500 | 15.00% |
| 50,000 | 9,203.00 | 18.40% | 11,127 | 22.25% |
| 100,000 | 23,528.50 | 23.53% | 26,522 | 26.52% |
| 500,000 | 174,528.50 | 34.90% | 178,772 | 35.75% |
| 1,000,000 | 372,528.50 | 37.25% | 376,772 | 37.68% |

The alternative minimum tax rate was increased to 26 per cent for incomes less than 175,000, but at incomes over 175,000 the rate was increased to 28 per cent.

Over the last few years the Congress seems to be troubled by the continuing Federal budget deficits, but not troubled enough to do anything about actually reducing the deficit or even having a plan for curtailing the continually growing Federal Debt.

The Congress added a new wrinkle—the phasing out of the personal exemption starting at a taxable income over $162,700 and completely phased out at $285,200 for married taxpayers filing joint returns and starting the phase out at 108,450 and completely phasing out at $230,950 for single taxpayers. Personal exemptions were $2,350 each.

For 1994 there was a slight reduction in taxes and the computed taxes are listed below:

| Taxable Income | Joint Return Taxes | | Single Return Taxes | |
|---|---|---|---|---|
| 10,000 | 1,500.00 | 15.00% | 1,500.00 | 15.00% |
| 50,000 | 9,060.00 | 18.12% | 11,042.50 | 22.08% |
| 100,000 | 23,304.50 | 23.30% | 26,389.50 | 26.39% |
| 500,000 | 174,304.50 | 34.86% | 175,639.50 | 35.12% |
| 1,000,000 | 372,304.50 | 37.23% | 373,639.50 | 37.36% |

Phasing-out of personal exemptions started at $157,900 and was completely phased out by $284,000 for joint returns, and for single returns phase-out started at $105,250 and complete phase out occurred at $227,750. For higher income taxpayers this was a sly way of increasing their taxes.

With all the tinkering with taxes, the Congress has not come close to balancing the Federal budget in any of the last twenty five years. Evidently their economists and other advisors haven't told the Congress how important a positive investment climate is to the economic growth of the country. With higher economic growth, Federal tax revenues grow and when the growth is great enough, Federal tax revenues flow into the Government at higher and higher rates, so that eventually it will become possible to balance the budget and even create surpluses.

With no loud and serious complaints, Congress could spend whatever their constituents seemed to want, and there appeared to be no restriction or limit to the requirements of their constituents. The most consistent pressure on each and every Senator and Congressman was very simple: Be sure to get re-elected! Ignore the towering Federal Debt, forget the ever increasing Federal Deficit; so what, the country was spending much more than it took in revenues. Congressman and Senators didn't have to worry about the future, the most important thing was now and get reelected. Let someone else worry about the future. Why worry about falling productivity why worry about low economic growth, why worry about unemployment, why worry about low savings rates, why worry about the falling value of the Dollar against other world currencies. The furious spending year after year, with no responsibility for the ultimate consequences, led to our current terrible economic stature, incredible Federal Debt, continuing Federal Deficits, weakening currency, and low international competitiveness. Beside the runaway spending, Federal Tax Policy established by completely ignorant economists, and totally un-knowledgeable legislators has lowered the nation's savings rate, lowered its investment rate, and reduced the United States to an also-ran economic power. In late 1996 the Japanese economy will approach that of the United States—only 50 years after Japan was defeated in World War II and had its productive capability reduced significantly to almost complete impotence. It is interesting to find that the Japanese tax polices motivated the people of that country to save and invest three to four times that of the people of the United States. That tax policy will propel Japan to grow into the largest economic power in the world.

CHAPTER SEVEN

# Research at the National Archives Letters from Concerned Citizens for Years 1969–70 Limited by Law

## *Research at the National Archives*

The author was determined to search the files of the National Archives to find critical concerns of citizens regarding the management of our fiscal and tax policies. The author found that there was a prohibition against releasing any correspondence from citizens to the House of Representatives for 30 years and a prohibition against releasing letters from citizens to the Senate for 25 years. The author was appalled that such prohibitions were in place, but decided to research the Senate Finance Committee correspondence during the 1969–1970 time period.

The author found a number of letters from concerned citizens who at that time were concerned about both tax policy and fiscal policy. These letters are contained in the following section of the book.

It must be remembered that these letters were sent in the 1969 to 1970 time period. The concerns expressed at that time showed a considerable mistrust of the policies of the Federal Government, and a concern that changes must be made to reverse the trends in national economic performance. Some were worried about the continual Federal Deficits, some were concerned about the tax policies as they were, and others were concerned about the trend of federal spending.

Some were even concerned that the Government was guilty of fraud. Another was convinced that there was a secrecy policy in the Internal revenue Service that led to abuses of civilian rights under the Constitution.

What is interesting to contemplate is what those same citizens would think now that 25 or 26 years have passed and the Federal Deficits have exceeded even their worst predictions, and Federal Debt has risen to incomprehensible levels.

The years prior to 1969 were the most productive years in the nation's history, real economic growth had for nine years averaged 4.335 per cent per year, there was a positive international trade balance, unemployment was at an all-time low, the nation experienced a federal surplus, and the nation was the most productive in the world. The United States was the most powerful country in the world economically, militarily, and socially.

The sense of the letters from concerned citizens was that there was a serious problem impending, and they could see that there was a trend in national policies that were not in the best long range interests of the country. It is only conjecture to extrapolate their concerns into the present day problems of high unemployment, continuing Federal Deficits, and the now incomprehensible Federal Debt.

Although we cannot be privy to the letters that are being received now and in the last 25 years, it would be interesting to expose the letters that are now being received by the House of Representatives and the Senate, with financial problems much more serious now than in 1969, our country's citizens must be writing letters of concern that are much more critical of our national policies than those of 25 years ago.

As you will read in the letters of concerned citizens during 1969, the problems then were real, and 25 years of history will not erase those problems. Actually those problems have gotten much worse in the years following 1969. The solutions to some of those problems is the purpose of this book.

## *The Former and Prospective Resident of Louisiana Writes:*

"I am writing to express my views on current tax issues and the related matter of government economies.

"I believe that the surtax is a fair tax applying equally to all and that it should be extended for whatever time is needed to reduce inflation.

"On the other hand, I feel a great concern about some of the so-called tax reforms now under consideration. The initial intent seemed to be directed toward a few people who have incomes of $200 thousand to over $1 million annually and who pay no tax. However, many of the currently proposed reforms will have the effect of increasing taxes on a very large group of middle- and upper- income people who are already carrying a very high burden of taxation relative to their incomes.

"In particular, I object very strongly: to increasing tax rates on lump sum settlements of pension programs or on deferred compensation. Future pension changes will greatly affect the future retirement of everyone with whom I work, and cause some to retire now. I am also much concerned about the adverse effects of increasing taxes on capital gains on investments. This atmosphere of increasing taxation is creating much uncertainty and reducing incentives for future investments.

"It seems to me that a great deal more attention should be given to reducing the cost of Federal functions instead of increasing taxes. I commend your efforts to date to re-examine priorities and reduce some programs to make room for new needs or reduce taxes. However, I also feel that there is a great opportunity to carry out many of the present programs at lower personnel and administrative costs. In short, I feel that many Federal functions have too many people for the job.

"It has been my experience that competition continually forces business to effect economies in staff. I do not see sufficient evidence of this in governments. I believe it can be done, but requires a continual effort of management attention to each job and person—to simplify and combine jobs, eliminate unnecessary procedures, separate unneeded people, and avoid hiring. Budgets alone cannot do the job—continual review of personnel trends is necessary.

"It is my opinion that no organization, either public or Private, will make the effort to effect economies without strong action from the top. In government this means strong and continued efforts from the legislative and top executive levels. I hope a re-examination of such efforts will be linked with surtax extension.

"I hope these views will be of some help to you in your responsibilities. My best wishes to you for continued good work.

Sincerely,
F. A. L. Holloway

"P.S. My wife and I are former and prospective future residents of Louisiana."

Mr. Holloway was right on when he zeroed in on the so-called "Tax Reform" which started the economic decline of the United States. The Tax Reform Act of 1969 fouled up the investment climate with not only tax increases on investment but with added significant uncertainties clouding up the investor's vision and perception when contemplating an investment decision.

## *A Concerned and Confused Taxpayer*

On February 20, 1970 Senator Russell B. Long was sent a letter from William N. Bret, Jr. vice president of a consulting firm in Dallas, Texas in which Mr. Bret addresses Senator Long as Sir:

**Tax Reform Act of 1969**

"While there were tax inequities in the past that needed correction, this act seems to be very damaging to the managerial class in the United States. This is accomplished by reducing the advantages of qualified stock option plans through its tax preference item, a 10% tax on seven other preferences including investment interest, capital gains and depletion, its seven-year averaging rule on pension and profit sharing distributions after January 1, 1970, its practical elimination of restricted stock plans, and the drawing together of the capital gains tax and the tax on earned income.

"The new law will tend to discourage executives from assuming responsibilities and taking risks with their capital. It will tend to discourage the new investment of individual savings in real estate, farms, new businesses, and in fact, make the stock market itself a less attractive vehicle for investment.

"The bill is so difficult to understand that it is almost incomprehensible even to qualified tax counsel and will be years before the regulatory bodies decide just what is meant by many of the provisions. Can it be that these matters are too complex for legislative solution under the present committee system?

"Your comment on this will be greatly appreciated since we have many clients bemused and wondering.

Very truly yours,
A. S. Hansen, Inc.
William N. Bret, Jr.
Vice President"

Mr. Bret certainly made his point that the complexity of the law led to uncertainty for the investor, which is the most important effect, but also led to confusion of all the taxpayers. While the Tax Reform Act of 1969 was the first step in making our tax laws less and less moral, the 1976, 1984 and 1986 laws have made our Internal Revenue Code so completely inunderstandable, that less and less people are making that most critical of all decisions for the country: should I invest or should I consume? When that critical decision is pushed in the direction of consumption, the nation suffers from low economic growth, unemployment, lower creation of new technology, lower rate of introduction of new products, negative international trade balances, continuing Federal Deficits, and eventually an insurmountable Federal Debt. If the individual's decision is motivated toward investment, rather than consumption, the economy grows, new jobs are created, new technologies are developed, more new products are introduced, Federal tax revenues increase, productivity improves, and the United States becomes more competitive in world markets, our balance of trade improves, and eventually Federal Deficits are eliminated and the government can start reducing the horrendous Federal Debt. This is not empty theory, but is based on economic history from 1960 to the present. But economic history must be studied in the proper manner, it must be studied over long terms with important policies' changes being fully understood. That is another reason for this book.

## *A Farmer Discusses Federal Spending*

John E. Kimber a California farmer wrote to Senator Russell B. Long on August 1, 1969 urging him to use "every influence you have" to control Federal spending. He also complained about the tax situation becoming "too heavy for taxpayers to bear."

Mr. Kimber also suggested that defense expenditures be reduced "without jeopardizing the safety of the nation," and "welfare should be held to a reasonable amount," but entirely out of character, "Farm subsidies should be discontinued entirely."

He also suggested that since we have landed a man on the moon "it's time to slow up on expenditures for space exploration." And as for foreign aid it "should be scaled down somewhat because the people are carrying too heavy a tax load."

He said, "Most of the programs proposed for the betterment of People have merit but I don't think there is any justification for spending as much as is being asked for these programs."

Mr. Kimber concluded with, "I hope you will spend the people's money more frugally at this time. We have too fine and great a country to permit it to be destroyed by unrestrained extravagance." Here is a man who truly is interested in the future of his country. He was terribly upset by what he perceived to be uncontrolled spending of our Federal government and a heavy tax load upon the people.

Along the same lines an old friend of Senator Long's wrote on July 15, 1969, from Fort Lauderdale, Florida:

"Dear Russell:

"Here's your old L.S.U schoolmate spouting off again. It now appears, from the press, that you have 'sold out' to Mr. Nixon on the tax matter. You know how the situation is over home (Louisiana). I'd very much dislike having you do something which would not lighten the tax burden of all my family over there. Besides, whatever you do for them will also effect me down here, indirectly.

"May I ask one question of you? For God's sake, when is the Federal going to quit its reckless spending, its cheating the people, the scare tactics, and when will it again be 'for the people and of the people'? We the people have absolutely no confidence in the forces which are running our country—that's how bad it is, believe it or not. This should be some grounds for serious thinking by all of you Congressmen. Please don't give in.

Sincerely,
Dr. Floyd M. Mizell"

Here again is a man who is concerned about the future of his country. He is concerned about the heavy tax load and the uncontrolled Federal spending. He has no specific solution to the country's problems but certainly is concerned about the trend of national performance.

Your author was not concerned in 1969 as these two gentlemen were, because at that time there was no indication that the situation was getting much worse. In the subsequent six years the difficulties became much more apparent—higher inflation, higher unemployment, low economic growth, higher interest rates, lower productivity growth, and serious negative trade balances. Those were six terrible years which established the downward trend of national performance, and by 1977 your author started his campaign to improve the investment climate in our country. This book is an extension of that campaign.

## *A Concerned Citizen Proposes a New Approach*

Mr. Walter C. Crain of Alexandria, Virginia wrote to Senator Russell B. Long on October 27, 1970 the following letter:

"Going back to your edifying tax article in the Washington Star, under date of April 16, 1967, under large headlines, it stated—'OUR TAX LAW IS UNFAIR.' The article contained the depressing statement that—'Some $100,000,000,000 of personal income, banked last year, probably will not be reported on Federal tax returns at all.' Also that—'One treasury study showed that 26 per cent of the taxpayers with adjusted gross incomes-of $5,000,000 each, paid no income tax at all.'

"As a layman in the business sector, and having to do with taxes in one way or another, since their inception in 1913, I have yielded to a personal urge to try to find a way out of this dilemma, a tax law you call 'unfair.' In my years of research and study, I have found the relief we seek, and have devised a plan by which darkness can be turned into day, if our tax planners, in Washington, will cast aside political expediency and make equitable, rational, simple and adequate tax relief of the overburdened tax payers of America their goal.

"For want of a better name, I have called this plan 'The Dollar Tax Plan.' It is predicated entirely upon the movement of the Dollar, the U.S. unit of measure in our monetary system. Just how many trillions of these dollars go from one owner to another each year to be recorded by each respective receiver, can only be determined by experience. When we take into consideration the trillions of dollars received and disbursed by entities and groups not taxable, it is incomprehensible.

"I realize my dear Senator you are a very busy man engrossed in the duties of your office and should not be imposed upon by matters that have no merit, but I too, have too much to do to plan a tax system, I would like to know at this point if the plan has merit, if not I will dismiss it from further study. If you will be kind enough to have one of your economic assistants go over the plan carefully and give me a frank report as to its shortcomings, it will be greatly appreciated.

"'Wishing you success in your current tax studies, I am

Yours very truly
W. C. Crain"

Mr. Crain was obviously upset by the tax laws as they were in 1970. His proposed plan to change the tax laws is presented below:

**THE DOLLAR TAX PLAN**
**A New and Radically Different Concept in Taxation**
**For Federal Revenue**

The DOLLAR TAX PLAN, as set forth herein, is proposed for use by the Federal Government to produce the additional revenue necessary to meet the unlimited needs of War and Peace. This would not be a tax as such, but rather a justifiable service charge for the use of the Federal Monetary System, spelled out in Dollars. The basis upon which it would rest would encompass the full and complete daily movement of Dollars, regardless of profit or loss or other consequent factors.

Each and every individual and entity of every kind, whatsoever, that receives Dollars or the equivalent thereof, from any source and for any purpose, in his own name, right, title, or delegated authority, would pay a service charge or tax to the Federal Government for the use thereof with no exceptions, no deductions or loopholes for evasion. Dollars measured in computerized billions would be exposed daily for tax assessment and payment. The rate of the service charge, per Dollar, would be determined, perhaps at two mills, one-fifth of one cent. This would be ample, equitable, justifiable, and certainly would not deter the active movement of Dollars in any situation.

A brief history of the Dollar gives added strength to its availability as a logical basis for use in the manner proposed herein. It was first issued and made the Federal Legal Tender by act of the Continental Congress in 1794. Over the years it has been maintained, stabilized and supported by the Federal Government as our only medium of exchange. It is the most stable monetary unit in use wherever business transactions occur. The point here is not so much to glorify the Dollar, but rather to emphasize the strategic position it occupies as a made to order tax base, available for immediate service in this present period of a National money crisis.

A limited summation of the grand total involvement of Dollars for the annual period, proposed for use under this plan, is such as to stagger the imagination. Incalculable trillions of turnover Dollars would beget billions of much needed revenue. At the same time, each individual tax return would be a simple statement of total Dollars received, for a given period, multiplied by the fixed rate. The need for highly trained tax experts would be a thing of the past. Also of vital importance would be an automatic "pay-as-you-go" tax return system. Large business and industrial corporations, financial, insurance and lending institutions, stock, bond and commodity markets, transportation of all kinds, utilities, sporting events and labor groups as well as State and Municipal bodies would report their Dollar receipts and pay the tax, monthly, quarterly, or semi-annually as the law required. Individual and the smaller returns would be made and the tax paid annually.

The adoption of a revenue system, unrelated to the income tax process, would in itself produce a number of worthwhile bonuses in the field of taxation:

1. Declare the 10% surcharge on income taxes unnecessary.
2. Make income tax returns less urgent and allow more for study and enactment.
3. When the demand for extra revenue has subsided, the Dollar tax revenue, if applied to the National Debt, would pay the annual interest of some $20 billion and a substantial installment on the debt itself.

No attempt is made here to set forth the procedures, rules or regulations for the processing of this Dollar service charge system. These are the functions of management that come within the scope and responsibility of the Treasury Department. Due consideration would be given to the impact, if adopted, on current tax performance and integrated procedures established, pending the ultimate results produced by the new Dollar tax system. Finally, the most outstanding feature of this plan is the fact that a very large portion of the new revenue will come from individuals and sources never having contributed to the cost of Government before."

Mr. Crain certainly had done some advanced thinking to arrive at such a novel approach to the collecting of taxes. Since it is now 1995 it is apparent that Senator Long and the Finance Committee did not do anything to employ this novel approach to solving the nation's financial and economic problems, now that the Federal Debt has reached $5 trillion and the annual interest is near $240 billion twelve times the $20 billion cited in Mr. Crain's tax plan!

## *A Concerned Citizen Discusses Inflation*

Robert M. Cole of Chicago, Illinois on August 1, 1969 wrote to Senator Russell B. Long Chairman Senate Committee on Finance the following:

"Dear Chairman Long:

"I sincerely request that you take a few minutes to personally review the enclosed comments with regard to inflation, and my suggestions for its correction. It will work. Let's act now!

Sincerely yours,
Robert M. Cole"

Mr. Cole also included a five-page document discussing the problem of inflation. Some of the cogent points made by Mr. Cole are presented below:

The law of Supply and Demand, i.e., when supply exceeds demand prices will decrease, when demand exceeds supply prices will rise. This is an easy to understand infallible law. Restraining money and credit reduces supply and creates scarcity, so prices rise. This is inflation!

When Federal taxes are increased money moves from the public to the government where it is all spent, whereas the Public would have saved, invested, and spent. The attendant lack of saving and investing reduces the available supply. This is inflation:

When the Federal Reserve System causes interest rates to rise, the added cost of borrowing are passed along to the consumer. This is inflation!

Labor unions demand ever-increasing wages to keep pace with the higher prices. This is inflation!

We have been too slow—in doing enough to create an adequate supply to meet demand. This is inflation!

Mr. Cole proposes an alternative:

### "A REALISTIC MONEY SUPPLY AND THE ENACTMENT OF TAX CONTROLS"

I. Reverse monetary **restraint** completely and instead pump enough money into the economy to drastically lower interest rates across the board. This can be done. This should be started at once. You might consider pegging the re-discount rate at say 3% for 2 years and give the Banks what they need. This will bring all other lenders (insurance companies, etc.) into competition and lower money costs all along the line.

II. Enact new Federal Tax Laws which will reward the producers of "Supply" with more profits if they **reduce** prices and, conversely, penalize who **increase** prices with higher taxes and lower profits through "Tax Controls." This **will** work. This will not create the problems of the World War II methods.

If No. II above isn't quite clear, I mean simply that a producer who keeps the status quo on prices would have the same Tax Treatment as he now has. The same producer, however, by **lowering** prices could earn a greater profit on the bottom line because of decreased taxes. On the other hand, those who raise prices will have a higher Tax Rate and high enough to lower their profits. This is "Tax Control." This is Anti-inflation. This will hurt no one and help everyone. This is the American way.

Mr. Cole thought the Unions should support such a program because a price reduction is equal to a raise in wages. (And do not forget the **value** of Pensions.)

Mr. Cole also recognizes that the investor is important because he helps the economy grow. This is anti-inflation—the average person would bless you.

Mr. Cole concluded with: "Will you please try to convince the Federal Reserve System that they should try to keep Supply slightly ahead of Demand. Demand will soon catch up. Along with this plea, let us make sure that their forecasting equipment is overhauled and 'fine tuned' to make this an All-Country Economy rather than a Big-City Economy. **THIS IS ANTI-INFLATION!**"

Mr. Cole was another concerned citizen who expressed his genuine displeasure with things as they are. He took the time to study and understand what he thought were the serious problems facing our nation. Again if he were to look at our country's current situation he would be appalled. At the time of Mr. Cole's letter, inflation had grown from an average of 1.78% in the nine years from 1959 to 1968 to 6% in 1969, but reached 12% in 1974. The United

States Merchandise Trade Balance in 1969 was positive $40 billion, the Federal Deficit was only $25.161 billion in 1968 and the corresponding Federal Debt was only $369.769 billion that same year. Imagine how upset Mr. Cole would be if he had foreseen the Federal Deficit of $220.725 billion and a Federal Debt of $2,132.913 billion by 1986!

The tragedy is that with all the concern of many of our good people no one seems to be able to get control of Government spending. Even the Congress in the Spring of 1995 would not pass the Balanced Budget Amendment to the Constitution and let the people decide what must be done to do what responsible legislators should be doing if they were accountable for their actions. Imagine needing a Constitutional amendment to force the legislators to do what they should be doing if they were acting with commensurate responsibility!

Senator Long seemed to be the recipient of many letters hoping to change the direction of the country's tax policies. A Mr. Angus Powell president of David M. Lea & Company, inc. wrote to Senator Long the following:

"Dear Senator Long:

"I hope that you, as chairman of the Joint Committee on Internal Revenue Taxation and the Senate Finance Committee, will take time to read the enclosed reprint of the talk I made on inflation which outlines a possible solution to this critical problem facing our Nation today.

"As a businessman, and as a father of four, I am deeply concerned about what inflation is doing to our country. All segments of our society—business, labor, and government—must accept responsibility for this problem and work together in effecting a permanent solution. I, for one, hope this can be done ... indeed it must be done.

Very truly yours,
Angus Powell
President"

Mr. Angus Powell was another concerned citizen who realized that his children would be saddled with the problems created by the current state of events. Inflation, unemployment, low economic growth and reduced productivity were all some of the problems that Mr. Powell perceived as problems of the future to be foisted on his children.

## *A Citizen Believes that Government is Guilty of Fraud*

Mr. W. Vaughn Ellsworth from Mesa, Arizona wrote the following letter to Harold E. Snyder Director Collection Division, U.S. Treasury Department, Internal Revenue Service:

"Dear Mr. Snyder;

"I have received from Congressman John Rhodes a copy of your refusal to supply me under the Freedom of Information Act a copy of the Internal Revenue Service Training Manual.

"I have requested this as an exhibit in my study I am preparing to show how the Internal Revenue Service is violating the Constitutional Law of the Land every day.

"By copy of this letter I am requesting my Congressman to obtain the requested manuals.

"It is manifestly against public policy to have these secret publications teaching government agents how to deprive and defraud citizens of their lawful rights.

Yours very truly,
W. Vaughn Ellsworth"

Mr. Ellsworth is not just worried about the high taxes and the continually growing Federal spending and the horrendous Federal Debt, but is seriously concerned about the government's intention to deprive citizens of their lawful rights, and even to defraud some citizens.

He believes that the Internal Revenue Service does indeed resort to fraud and deceit to deprive citizens of their lawful rights. This is a charge that the author does not believe he has ever encountered in all of his dealings with the Internal Revenue Service. This author has found the agents he has dealt with to be straight-forward, competent public servants attempting to do their job in the best way possible under the circumstances. Any disagreements have always been resolved in a workman-like manner, where the Internal Revenue

Code was referred to and interpreted in an intelligent and understandable way. The author has always found the personnel of the Service to be able, competent, and knowledgeable people, who were well trained in their positions of responsibility. Other people have had less favorable interactions with the Internal Revenue Service, and possibly Mr. Ellsworth has been one of those people.

One cannot blame the Internal Revenue Service for the sad state of our tax laws. The blame rests with the Congress and the administrations which have lost all sight of what made America the most powerful country in the world—the free enterprise system. Prior to 1969 our tax laws were very moral and coincided with life as it is lived. Ever since 1969 well-meaning economists and so-called tax experts have helped concoct a set of tax laws that penalize saving and investment and foster consumption of goods and services by the people. The immorality of not being able to deduct real costs of doing business is one aspect of the new tax laws that certainly makes it much more difficult to invest and take risks to provide the capital that is necessary to provide jobs for our ever-increasing population, to create new products, to improve productivity, to cause real economic growth, to improve our international trade balances, and eventually to provide tax revenues so that our Government can pay its bills, and even reduce the terrible Federal Debt.

## *On the Lighter Side*

Rube Goldberg was a cartoonist with a most outstanding and creative mind. His fame and fortune were made by drawing complex mechanisms to solve relatively simple problems. In fact the dictionary defines Rube Goldberg inventions as "accomplishing by extremely complex roundabout means what actually or seemingly could be done simply."

Rube Goldberg died in December of 1970, but his spirit lives on. His spirit can be found in an ingenious contraption exhibit at the Smithsonian Institution, but also in the Social-Security-Trade-Welfare bill now before the United States Senate.

Contrary to widespread belief, however, the Senate bill was not one of Goldberg's inventions. It just happens to be the sort of legislation Goldberg might have drafted if he were Chairman of the Senate Finance Committee.

As a final tribute to the departed Goldberg, columnist Dick West endeavored to explain how the Social-Security-Trade-Welfare bill works:

"Inflation (A) causes an increase in wages (B), which catches business in a cost-price squeeze (C), business raises prices (D), which outrages the consumer (E), and causes him to start buying cheaper foreign goods (F), the flood of imports engulfs the businessman (G), who then builds a fire under his senator (H), creating pressure for restrictions on shoe, oil, and textile imports (I), an old man fearing he will no longer be able to get cheap shoes, oil, and textiles, appeals for an increase in Social Security benefits (K), which touches the heart of the finance committee.

"In responding to the old man's plea, the committee votes to raise Social Security Taxes (M), which tightens the squeeze on the businessman (N), and increases the pressure for protectionist legislation (O), this pressure closes a loophole in import quotas (P), and opens an escape clause in embargoes (Q), creating alarm in the free trade bloc (R), the alarm arouses the consumer (S), who squawks to the president (T), who threatens a veto (U), this causes the committee to mollify the consumer with a program providing financial protection against catastrophic illness (V), these added benefits leave the veteran (W), at a disadvantage, bringing about a pension increase (X), plus extra aid to the aged, blind, and disabled (Y), whereupon the Finance Committee approves the Social Security-Trade-Welfare bill (X)-may Rube Goldberg rest in peace.

"The Rube Goldberg article was found in the National Archives along with a note from Charles J. Ross who had written to the Senate Finance Committee a letter received on December 16, 1970. In his note Mr. Ross says, 'Is it asking too much to get the Rube Goldberg out of tax bills? Every taxpayer is expected to (and should) prepare tax returns and pay his taxes as provided in revenue acts. But the 'Goldberg's in the laws do not make it easy for one to know what the law is or says.'

Sincerely,
Charles J. Ross"

That was in 1970 when the entire tax code was in one volume. Imagine Mr Ross's feeling if he were here today with a code that includes 14,700 pages of sections and regulations, plus all the court decisions and special letters from the Internal Revenue Service; 230,000 pages!

There is a move afoot to try to simplify the Internal Revenue Code. Some proponents hope for a "Flat Tax." There is no doubt that a flat tax would eliminate all the complexities and complications of the present code. It is estimated that $300 billion is spent on lawyers and accountants and tax specialists including the wasted time of individuals spending time to assemble all the facts to arrive at a proper tax return.

Studies of the effects of different tax policies indicate that taxpayers should be motivated to save and invest by positive provisions in the tax law. The critical decision by each and every taxpayer to save and invest rather than to consume is terribly important to the generation of total Federal Revenues. That critical decision is made almost every payday by individuals—should I invest and save, or should I spend and consume?

A brief analysis was made of several companies in different businesses, trying to assess the effect of that critical decision. The question is, "Should I invest in the company, or should I buy its products?" If people invest in the company the company can produce more products. Since the people who invest do not buy, prices go down for two reasons—there is more supply, and there is less demand. It results in more people having more products at lower prices, in other words the standard of living of everyone improves. The biggest benefactor is the Federal Treasury, revenues are increased because of the increased economic growth caused by the higher investment by individuals who chose to invest rather than consume.

## *Someone Cared about High Productivity*

The following letter was sent by Richard S. White, President of Automation Engineering Laboratory, Incorporated in Wilton Connecticut to Russell B. Long on July 10, 1969;

SUBJECT: NEEDED—A NATIONAL HIGH PRODUCTIVITY POLICY

The **ONLY** Constructive Antidote to Inflation

"Dear Mr. Long:

"Our country is currently following a national policy which must be of grave concern to you. Our present monetary policy cannot work constructively to the interests of the American people. It is a policy which appears confused and in error and based upon factors of a bygone age. The present monetary policy, which is at least tacitly supported by the Government, works directly against the only enduring solution to inflation—namely, Increased Productivity.

"You are in a very important position—one in which you can provide leadership to correct this situation. I would like to briefly put down a few points and then a few suggestions for your consideration. This subject matter is vital to our society. If we do not adequately understand our position and act realistically, we can change a strong economy into chaos.

"1. On January 28, construction drivers won a $57.60 **weekly raise** (more than a 1.25/hour **increase!**) in New York. Will high interest rates reverse this boost to inflation? We both know that short of a severe economic disorientation, interest rates will not reverse this boost. Interest rates may soften the market and possibly cause some unemployment—but labor is not going to reverse its wage position. **ONLY** increased Productivity can prevent this wage increase from being an inflationary increase.

"2. There simply is **only one way** to **deal** with the **causes of inflation constructively**. And that is to put our energies to work imaginatively to **fulfill the demand of a healthy, strong society**. Inflation results from the **cost** of providing goods and services—and from strong underlying demand. We **can** and **must** hold down the cost per unit of goods and service by higher productive output per hour. That is, we must **increase** the **productivity** of **all of our people** to **produce the goods and services which we are all demanding**. **THIS SHOULD BE OUR NATIONAL POLICY**. This is technologically entirely possible. What we need is a **NATIONAL HIGH PRODUCTIVITY POLICY**.

"3. One of our major problems as a nation is that the policies we are presently pursuing work diametrically against our best interests with regard to increasing productivity.

"4. High taxes and high interest rates only go to slow down and discourage increases of productivity. The negative effect on productivity is by far the more pronounced than the effect on consumer demand (and thus inflation is amplified further)—and the reason is quite simple—the increase of productivity involves RISK. Every business manager increasing his productivity has to gamble against the future, and the more unattractive we make that gamble, the less he can justify increases in productivity, which increases in turn are the absolute and only answer to the desires and needs of the American public. Hence, the policies we have been following are totally against the best interests of our people, as well as representing a considerable failure in effectiveness.

"5. In order to decide what policies we should have concerning inflation, we need to look clearly at the causes of inflation and we need to do this without pretense that these causes are going to disappear or change. Certainly, the most significant factor affecting inflation is our willingness to have continual substantial wage increases. It is not my purpose in this letter to evaluate whether these wage increases are constructive or not, but I do believe that we must recognize their continuity and that from both a political and economic viewpoint, the probability is 99% that they will continue over the years ahead. (Even if we had wage controls for a period—which is probably unwise—this is no long term solution to our ability to meet the demands and needs of our society.) It is really playing a dangerous game with our American economy to be tightening the credit of commerce, and thus **preventing** a productivity offset to growing labor rates—about which I shall make specific suggestions.

"6. The second major factor concerning inflation is that we have substantial demand from individuals who are enjoying a high standard of living. In my opinion the **continuity** of this demand (which derives from widespread comfortable income levels, plus substantial individual savings) is inadequately understood—which is why the monetary and fiscal attempts of the past few years to stop this demand are a virtual failure. Basically, we should be very grateful for this demand, but we must clearly understand that the **United States has inadequate productivity** at this time **to meet the demand** present within our country. And, in my opinion, it is a mistake to blame the war alone for inflation—when the war subsides, there are many social objectives to replace; abatement of the war will not reverse wage levels, the core of cost levels.

"7. Two additional factors which further go to increase prices are, of course, taxes on the one hand, and more recently, the continual increase of interest costs. There is substantial confusion in the theory that says inflation will be slowed down by increasing taxes (which is supposed to reduce effective purchasing power—but which in fact also adds to costs, and thus adds to inflation) and by increasing interest costs (which is supposed to reduce effective purchasing power —but which in fact also adds to costs, and thus adds to inflation). The people who advocate these steps don't seem to give much attention to the correlative effect of these increased costs which compare with continued wage increases, in terms of the effect on the cost of goods and services. The fact is none of these three purchasing power retardants (higher wages, interest or taxes) are very effective within a tolerable and reasonable degree of restraint on our people. The costs which are encountered in commerce are ultimately passed on to the buyers—this is an ipso facto, irrevocable truth—or the enterprises providing the goods and services would go into bankruptcy. The further fact is that we have a sufficiently dynamic and underlying strong economy (including widespread comfortable income levels, plus substantial individual savings) so that all these costs are passed on, and the higher costs then experienced by the consumers, who are also wage earners, create further impetus for additional wage hikes.

"8. It is, of course, probably true that at some level, taxes and/or interest costs can cause a major economic disorientation which can be just as difficult to manage and prevent from getting out of hand as has been our questionable attempts to slow prosperity.

"9. Mr. Long, in my opinion, it is a grave error to think that we can 'fine tune' 200 million people to just the amount of buying that the economists would have them do. The theories that we are pursuing are drawn out of the past when people had very little reserves to fall back on, and when people did not have their present dynamic position for bargaining for their relative well-being.

"10. What we are trying to do via the tax and monetary routes is to tell our people to reduce their demand—that of course is a most **negative** policy. What all of the American people would like to see their leaders do, is rather to indicate **how** we can fulfill their demands. The demands are not going to decrease either politically or economically, nor in the person of the 'individual'—be he consumer—voter—or wage earner. The only constructive way, to meet the demand that exists in our market places, is a **NATIONAL POLICY TO INCREASE PRODUCTIVITY**—the only policy which is fundamentally sound if we are to continue to be successful at home and in the international economy.

"11. We should have the courage to recognize the strengths of buying power that are fundamental to our economy—and to be grateful for them—and to reverse our policies regarding high interest rates and tight money supply. We should revert to a substantially growing supply of low cost money, first of all. This is the only policy that will enable the fundamental growth of productivity that is a must. We should consider the possibility of selectivity in the extension of credit, giving particular priority to the use of funds to increase productivity. Subsequently, we could gradually reduce the tax rate which gradually will also increase the total amount of taxes received by the government, as our economy continues to grow. When these steps have been established as national policy and communicated as part of a New **NATIONAL HIGH PRODUCTIVITY POLICY**, the entrepreneurs in our country will quickly solve the problems of supply and demand which cannot be otherwise effectively legislated.

"Mr. Long, I have written this letter quite directly and specifically because of a high respect for you. I suspect that you are far too interested in sound performance to be wed to policies of the past which are no longer adequate for the economic well-being and strength and health of our country. You of course are in a most pivotal position to cause the adoption of a NATIONAL HIGH PRODUCTIVITY POLICY. You of course are in a position to introduce new legislation, and it may be that we have reached a time when it is essential to modify the laws governing the Federal Reserve System. Perhaps even more important, you can influence others concerning the need for new policies to promote productivity as the only viable basic solution to the causes of inflation. I shall most earnestly hope that this matter has your urgent attention.

"It is possible that my insights and experience (which include banking as well as industrial and technological experience) could be useful to you in your formulation of a strong position regarding this subject. I would be pleased to meet with you or help in any way you might believe I could.

"After you have read this letter, I would certainly appreciate knowing your reaction.

"With very best wishes and highest regards,

Sincerely yours,
Richard S. White"

Mr. White was certainly someone who cared enough to try to get something done to improve the unhealthy condition of our country in 1969. The previous year the Federal Deficit was $25.161 billion and the Federal Debt was $369.769 billion. Imagine how concerned Mr. White would have been if he had known that the Federal Deficit would grow to $220.725 billion and the Federal Debt to $2,132.913 billion by 1986!

## *Another Person Who Cared*

On November 6, 1970 the following was received from a concerned taxpayer by the Senate Committee on Finance: "Taxes for all levels of government now take over 35% of total national income. Consequently we are losing our character as a free enterprise economy and are becoming a "State" oriented and controlled economy.

This is socialism, which was not contemplated by the Declaration of Independence, nor intended under the Constitution.

Inflation in the U.S. is primarily the result of Government spending, or giving away money it does not have, and then paying for it by creating short term debt by selling short term treasury certificates. But it cannot repay these in the absence of a budgetary surplus. Therefore it refinances these certificates by issuing longer term obligations which become the equivalent of printing press money in circulation.

Credit restraints have thus far failed to stop the spiral of inflation because they treat the symptoms and not the disease. And if they are continued they may well bring on a real depression.

Legal wage and price controls were effective during the second World War because of the increased demand for military hardware. But under today's conditions they would lead to increased unemployment due to the slowing down of business activity and the high minimum wage laws.

Currency devaluation in many countries in the past has resulted from excess inflation—spending more than the tax take. It has often been adopted as a means of wiping out excessive printing press money in circulation and the public debt it represented.

In the U.S. the depreciated value of the dollar (in its purchasing power) has already wiped out billions of hard-earned purchasing power represented by savings bank deposits, life insurance policies, endowment and trust funds.

Corrective measures must rest on a determination to reduce Federal spending to a point well below the tax-take each year. This can be done if the Congress will count the dollars involved in legislative acts instead of the votes that come as a result of those legislative acts.

Then the Federal Debt and the tax rates may be reduced year by year until the national debt is manageable without requiring such high coupon rates.

Then the labor laws should be modified to put labor unions under the anti-trust laws and to give every man the right to work at a trade without joining a union.

Then the Federal minimum wage laws should be abolished as they restrict the hiring of the young."

These are the views of a concerned citizen who has been frustrated by what he perceives to be a government out of control, unresponsive to the needs of the people for sound economic policies that would benefit all the people. At least he tried by writing to the Senate Committee on Finance, but that was 1970, before our country took a terrible turn for the worse with high inflation, high unemployment, high interest rates, low economic growth, and sliding international trade balances. That concerned citizen deserves credit for his perspicacity in foreseeing the difficulties our country would face in the years to come. That concerned citizen was Lindsay H. Whelling.

## *A Citizen Objects to Taxes*

On January 28, 1982 the author received a letter from a Ph.D. Gunnar Bergman who had had a conversation with the author in the previous year concerning the author's efforts to reduce the capital gains tax rate. Dr. Bergman had worked diligently to arrive at a system of taxation that would be more equitable for all taxpayers.

Bergman discussed the inequities in taxing corporations:

1. If a corporation's taxes are increased, the corporation can raise prices to account for the tax increase, and since all people pay those increased prices, even the poorest people pay for the added taxes. Such a burden is inequitable.
2. If a corporation's taxes are increased, and the corporation cannot raise prices, the shareholders who receive less income really pay the added taxes, this is inequitable since other taxpayers who are not shareholders are free of that tax.

Bergman concludes that corporation taxes based on income should be abolished, because of the inescapable inequities.

Bergman also discussed the inequities in the personal income tax. As an example he considered two taxpayers having the same income. One is a spender and saves nothing, the other saves a large part of his income. Under present tax law both taxpayers pay the same tax. The saving taxpayer denies himself the immediate gratification of spending for goods and services for his own consumption or enjoyment, but adds to the capital stock of the country to be used by corporations for the benefit of its employees, customers, and shareholders. The saving taxpayer should not be forced to pay tax on the part of his income he has invested. Tax on the saver should be due when the taxpayer withdraws his invested funds and spends them on goods and services for his own consumption and enjoyment.

Bergman concludes that taxes on personal income lead to inequities and should be abolished. He also pointed out that there were important consequences of his proposed new system of taxation.

Bergman listed the eight consequences of his taxation procedure:

1. There is no capital gains tax.
2. There are no depreciation allowances.
3. There are no depletion allowances.
4. Increased incentives to save and invest.
5. Discouragement of investments made only to avoid taxes.
6. Freeing up capital now "locked in."
7. Eliminates the double taxation of corporation income.
8. IRA, Keogh, SEP plans are not needed.

What Bergman has proposed is a total revision of the way taxes are perceived, computed, and collected. Certainly he has tried to correct what are the complications and complexities of the present system of taxation. In his letter he stated he was well aware of the immense problems facing any effort to achieve a major change of the type he had in mind. "Perhaps the battle can only be won in steps ... a taxation procedure that also contains strong incentives to save and invest. A very desirable by-product!"

CHAPTER EIGHT

# Sometimes We are Misled by Unknowing People

## *One of the Misleaders*

Joseph J. Minarik Executive Director for Policy and Chief Economist, U.S. House of Representatives Committee on the Budget had an article entitled, "Capital Gains Taxation, Growth, and Fairness" in Contemporary Policy Issues Vol. X July 1992.[4]

Mr. Minarik's conclusion:

"Policy-makers should not expect to resolve the capital gains issue on the basis of any one criterion of tax policy. Like any tax policy choice, capital gains taxation is multidimensional, and policy-makers must weigh each option's advantages and disadvantages.

"A capital gains tax break would increase personal saving infinitesimally if at all, while it would decrease federal tax revenues and thus decrease national saving. It would have little impact on total investment, but it would almost certainly shift investment into low value commercial real estate and out of other, more productive uses. Its positive impact on risky investment projects most likely will not be significant. Thus, the net impact on economic growth would likely be negative. At the same time, a capital gains tax preference would reduce the taxes of the most well-to-do members of society. It would reopen broad avenues for abuse and complicate economic decisions."

Is it any wonder that our country has continued to have federal deficits when the House of Representatives Director of Policy for the Committee on the Budget and Chief Economist arrives at the above conclusion! What kind of legislative advice has he been giving to the Committee on the Budget? If such advice is based on the conclusions he has advanced, the Committee on the Budget has been seriously misled.

If Minarik had looked over a period of 32 years he might have come to a much more reasonable analysis of economic data. With the top income tax rate at 91 per cent in the 1960 to 1969 period, the capital gains tax rate was at 25 per cent. Real economic growth in that period averaged 4.335 per cent per year and annual productivity increases averaged 3.23 per cent per year. The United States enjoyed a positive merchandise trade balance in 1969, and that was the last year that the U.S. had a budget surplus. The Tax Reform Act of 1969 reduced the top tax rate on income from 91 to 70 per cent, but that raised the capital gains tax rate from 25 per cent in 1969 to 29.5 and 32.5 per cent in 1970 and 1971, respectively. That act also added a minimum tax of 10 per cent, so that at the highest levels of capital gains the top rate was 42.5 per cent.

In the next six years Real Economic Growth dropped to 1.557 per cent per year, and Annual Productivity Increases dropped to 1.529 per cent per year. That is not an economists prediction but the true history of what happened. By 1976 Federal Deficits grew to $73.719 billion and since have continued to grow. Most economists predicted that a cut in the top income tax rate would be beneficial to the economy and perhaps it was, but no economists predicted the horrible results of increasing the tax on capital gains. In spite of cuts in income tax rates, which should have been a positive development for the economy, the increase in the capital gains tax over-powered the beneficial effects of the cut in income tax rates.

Other horrible results were the growth in unemployment, and the loss of equity investment. 1800 companies went to the equity market for new equity capital in 1969, by 1975 only 150 companies went to the equity market. The numbers are even worse for small companies. For companies having less than $5 million net worth, 649 were able to raise equity capital in 1969, but by 1974 only 9 companies were able to raise new equity capital

What was even worse, 200 technical companies were able to raise capital in 1969, and by 1975 only 2 technical companies were able to raise equity capital. A Department of Commerce report issued in December 1976 showed that small companies created new jobs at a rate 66 times faster than very large companies, because of their faster rate of growth. The loss of available venture capital had a serious consequence in reducing the flow of new technology, in causing a rising tide of unemployment, and in slowing the growth of productivity.

Mr. Minarik obviously has not seen the above data, because if he had there is no way he could conclude that the taxation of capital gains is unimportant to sound tax policy. The record is clear, even though ordinary income tax rates were reduced significantly, the increase in the capital gains tax to a maximum of 42.5 per cent from 25 per cent completely over-powered the effect of other income tax rate reductions.

The long term effects of the Tax Reform Act of 1969 have been astounding: Merchandise trade balances falling from a positive 40 billion to a negative 50 billion or more, Real Economic Growth falling from 4.335 per cent per year to a little over 2 per cent. Federal Deficits in all the years since 1969, the last year that any Federal surplus was experienced. Unemployment rising from 3.5 per cent of the work force to as high as 10 per cent and hovering near 6 or 7 per cent year after year.

Mr. Minarik should learn that tax policy should motivate taxpayers to invest in the future of their country to create Real Economic Growth, new technology, new products, new jobs, and most critical of all more tax revenues so that the government can pay its bills, reduce deficits, and eventually pay down the horrendous Federal Debt.

Many of the complexities of the present Internal Revenue Code create such uncertainty, that those uncertainties alone deter investment by private individuals. Coupled with the relatively high rate of tax on capital gains, and the restrictions on the deduction for investment interest, and the inability to write off significant capital losses, the risk-to-reward ratio is so high that it also de-motivates individuals to invest and take risks.

Another conclusion reached by Minarik that a capital gains tax break would increase individual savings infinitesimally if at all is pure false conjecture, and his further conclusion that it would decrease tax revenues is contradicted by what actually happened after the cuts in capital gains tax rates in 1978 through 1980. History shows that revenues increased substantially after those tax cuts. His further conclusion that such a cut in capital gains tax rates would have little impact on total investment is also false, as prior data above has shown that increases in the capital gains tax rate dried up venture capital, and drove even large corporations to the debt markets for their sorely needed new capital, and that drove interest rates up to as high as 16 per cent.

Minarik's further conclusion that the net impact on economic growth would be negative is totally false. As the increases in capital gains tax rates in 1969 and 1976 caused reduced investment, economic growth dove from 4.335 per cent per year to less than 2 per cent per year. Minarik's credentials as a policy director and Chief Economist are suspect when we examine his conclusion. "It would reopen broad avenues for abuse and complicate economic decisions." The current tax code is so complex and confusing that it already complicates economic decisions, a simple 11.5 per cent rate for long term capital gains with no complications of the minimum tax would certainly simplify the tax code and remove the uncertainties associated with making an investment.

Minarik raises the question, "The real issue is whether taxing some people at a different rate than others having the same income level is appropriate." By emphasizing this so-called principle of taxation Minarik shows his true colors. He obviously thinks there is no difference Between people who save and eventually risk their capital with the possibility of gain or loss and those who generate income from work and other sources of ordinary income. He does not realize how important it is to motivate people to take risks to invest and to create new technology, new products, new jobs, and real economic growth, and with that growth added tax revenues to permit the government to be able to pay its bills and eventually reduce the terrible Federal Debt.

He even brings up the possibility of taxing capital gains on the accrual basis, one of the worst possible methods of taxation—demanding that an investor pay taxes on gains that have not been realized each year he remains invested. He even indicates that such an alternative would be extremely attractive if it could be obtained. He may not realize it but that method of taxation is the worst of any of his proposals.

In one statement he correctly states that faster economic growth requires additional capital formation, but later concludes that a cut in the capital gains tax rate would drive up interest rates—a totally false conclusion. The cut in ordinary rates from 91 per cent to 70 per cent should have been beneficial to the economy. The increase in long term capital gains tax rates from 25 per cent to 42.5 per cent, when the effect of the minimum tax are added to the capital gains tax, caused equity investment to drop significantly, as previously indicated,and interest rates eventually reached 16 per cent as corporations were forced to go to the debt markets to raise sorely needed capital to continue to invest in new equipment and in new products.

If this article by Mr. Minarik is any indication of the spread of his ideas and his concepts of what is proper tax policy for our country, it is easy to conclude why our country has not been able to reduce its continuing Federal Deficits, and has not been able to balance its annual budget. If such advice is continued, it is clear that the country will never solve its financial and economic problems.

The current Federal Debt of $5 trillion is a national disgrace as is the lack of responsibility of our legislators and our administrations to have the courage to establish tax and other policies to carry out their intentions to produce a balanced budget. The legislators and the administration turned down the balanced budget amendment—imagine the total lack of responsible action to create a constitutional amendment to force the legislators to do what they should have been doing over the last 26 years. Remember the last Federal budget surplus was reached in 1969. 26 Years of irresponsible action of legislators and administrations has driven our Federal Debt to its current horrendous level. Is it that they didn't care?

Perhaps they have been the victims of continuing bad advice of staff members and advisors to the various committees of the House of Representatives and of the Senate. There is no doubt that some really did care, some really did try to improve the policies of our country.

## *Phillips's Folly*

There is an economist named Phillips who supposedly constructed a curve and called it the Phillips's Curve. The curve was simply a relationship between Inflation and Unemployment. According to some economists who believe in the Phillips's Curve, when an economy has high inflation it will usually have low unemployment, and when there is low inflation there will be high unemployment. Obviously, Phillips must have been making a case for continued high unemployment, so that inflation would be under control. Or he could have been arguing that if you want low unemployment, you would get high inflation. The curve looks like the accompanying figure.

An economist came to my office one day when I was President of Beckman Instruments, Inc. and cited "The Phillips's Curve." And he also made the above arguments. It occurred to me that Phillips had taken his data in a relatively stable investment climate. If he did, there truly is A Phillips Curve. The unfortunate thing is that there are many differing investment climates. As the investment climate improves the entire curve moves down and to the left, and as the investment climate deteriorates the curve moves upward and to the right. In fact there are an infinite number of Phillips Curves, each one depending upon the existing investment climate.

To demonstrate my conclusion that the Phillips's Curve does change with differing investment climate, the tax law of 1954 brought into being the best investment climate this country has seen in the last fifty years. The accompanying data are shown for the years 1954 through 1969. Then when the investment climate

# The Erroneous "PHILLIPS CURVE" Effect of the Investment Climate Upon Inflation and Resulting Unemployment

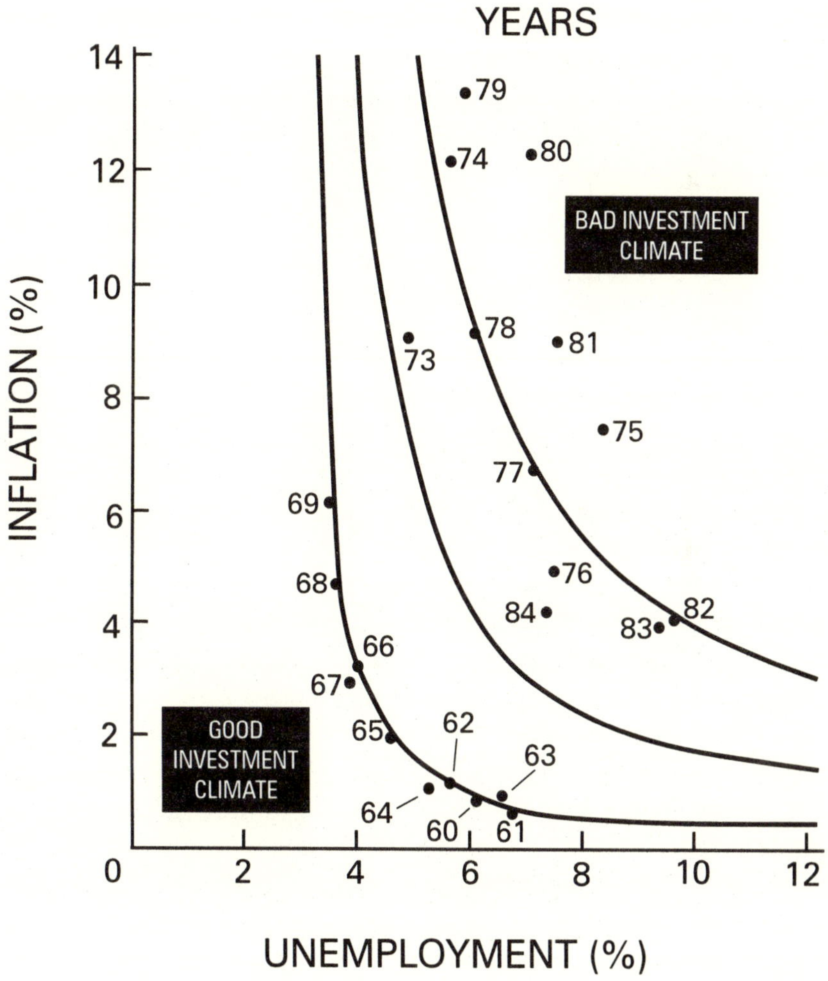

was fouled by the 1969 Tax Reform Act, the data show the different so-called Pillip's Curve far to the right and much higher than when the investment climate was at its best in the 1954 to 1969 time period.

Tax policy has a profound effect on the people who work and exist in the economic environment. Erroneous tax policy also has a profound effect upon the investment climate. The connection between tax policy and investment climate is real and not some dream or theory, the facts are there to be read by thinking people. Tax policy has caused the serious degradation of United States Economic Power in the World. Tax policy of our international competitors has allowed them to improve their relative economic power over that of the United States: and that is not a dream or empty theory, that is REAL!

## *View from Washington*

James Risen writes about the economy from the Los Angeles Times Washington bureau. In the August 6, 1995 Los Angeles Times Mr. Risen created an article entitled, "Maybe, Just Maybe, American Workers Can Stage A Comeback."[5] Some of the concepts outlined in the article indicate some of the fallacies and misunderstandings of many economists.

One of the paragraphs stated, "Average wages, adjusted for inflation, have been steadily declining while labor productivity—one of the best measures of corporate efficiency—has been steadily rising. The gap between the two has widened by at least two percentage points for two straight years." The fallacy in this statement has a correction to the wages paid for inflation but has no correction in the level of labor productivity for inflation. If there is any inflation both wages and labor productivity should be adjusted for inflation.

"What we are seeing today is not unprecedented," said one Administration Economist who asked not to be identified by name. "In the past, there have been many times when we have experienced gaps between the growth of productivity and the growth of wages that were similar to what we see now."

Later that same economist stated, "... the economic data tends to overstate the real gap between productivity and wages. The government doesn't use the same inflation-adjustment formulas to adjust productivity as it does to figure inflation's impact on wage growth. The consumer price index is used to adjust wages, while the GDP deflator, a different measure of inflation, is used to adjust productivity for inflation."

He further stated, "Still, that doesn't mean that the historic link between productivity and wages—one that has kept the two more or less in line—has now been broken."

Nowhere in the article does that author discuss the most important consideration in any jobs, wages, and productivity discussion—the importance of the personal, private investment climate. A poor investment climate means less motivation to take risks and invest to create jobs, to improve productivity, to create real economic growth, and to drive inflation down. More personal private investment will create more jobs and products for our ever-growing population. When more products are available, that means more SUPPLY—and greater supply of goods drives prices down. The people who are motivated to invest, by that critical decision have chosen to defer consumption, that means less DEMAND—and less demand means lower prices. The people who have been put to work by the creation of the new jobs will be able to afford to buy the ever increasing flow of products at the newly reduced prices. The increased real economic growth caused by increased personal private investment will result in substantial growth in tax receipts so the government can pay its bills without further borrowing, and if there is enough investment the increased real economic growth could lead not only to a balanced budget, but eventually to a reduction of the total Federal Debt!

This author has found that the American Worker is the best in the world, but he is saddled with a government that has created a monstrous tax policy that is complex, complicated, not well understood, and such a deterrent to investment that the worker is the one who suffers. American workers don't have to come back! They are already there, the House and the Senate should change tax policy to motivate people to invest in the future of their country by the millions!

## *A Federal Reserve Board Economist Writes*

Mr. Brian Motley Senior Economist for the Federal Reserve Bank of San Francisco in the February 5, 1993 issue of the FRBSF Weekly Letter published an article entitled, "The Sources of the Growth Slowdown."[6]

Most economists like Mr. Motley study data over years that have no significant importance. For instance Sources of Economic Growth in Industrial Countries was presented for five industrial countries; United States, United Kingdom, Germany, France, and Japan. The span of years used for comparison was 1962 to 1974, and later from 1975 to 1985. The conclusion from the data was that economic growth had slowed for all five countries. The confusing portion of the data was that Economic Growth was broken into three parts; that produced by labor, that produced by Capital, and that produced by Productivity.

Motley's contention was that increased labor supply contributed to economic growth, but was roughly the same for both the earlier and the later period. Certainly increased investment was necessary to increase the number of jobs, and consequently the increased labor supply. He also contends that capital and productivity contributed the most (as much as 90 per cent or more) to economic growth, in both the earlier and the later period. Motley, for some reason has tried to divide the contribution to economic growth into that caused by capital and that caused by productivity. This is confusing because productivity is directly related to investment, and capital should also be directly related to investment.

A 1977 study of the investment ratios of the United States, Germany and Japan showed a direct correlation of investment ratio with productivity growth per year over a period of thirteen years from 1960 to 1973. In other words, if you want to increase productivity, you must increase your investment ratio.

A further study of real economic growth over the nine years prior to 1969 and the six years after 1969, showed that real economic growth in the earlier period averaged 4.335 per cent per year, and in the later period averaged only 1.657 per cent per year. The critical change that was made in 1969 was the passage of the Tax Reform Act of 1969. That act so fouled up the investment climate that people reduced their levels of investment such that equity investment, and worst of all venture capital investment almost dried up completely.

Evidently economists are not alert to the significant changes in tax policy of the United States, the effects such policy has, not only upon the United States, but upon the economies of the entire world. Tax policy which reduces investment not only causes United States economic growth to slow but also, since the economy of the United States is so large with respect to the rest of the world, will slow the growth of the economies of the world. The United States is certainly a part of the international economy and has a tendency to drive the world's economy, whether we like it or not. Deeper study will confirm that the tax policies of the United States which made investment so much more difficult are really responsible for the world's growth slow-down. There is no doubt that investment creates economic growth, with new products, new technology, and new jobs. Undeveloped countries are only undeveloped because there is no capital that is essential to development. The combination of education, technology and capital investment is usually sufficient to provide the fuel to the engine of economic growth.

## *A Different Look at the Troubles of the United States*

In September 1986 Deborah S. Cohen a student intern working with the California Engineering Foundation completed a study, "Competitiveness In The United States, A Brief Review Of Research And Investigations."[7]

Some of the data presented in the study was taken from the Statistical Abstract of the United States 1986. As usual, the data were presented for five year periods with no consideration for the critical events that occurred in specific time periods.

The purchasing power of the dollar dropped from 1.25 in the 1955 time period to 0.31 by the 1985 time period.

The Federal budget deficit in the 1955 time period was 3.0 Billions and grew continually to 222 Billions by the 1986 time period.

The Federal Debt was 323 Billions in the 1965 time period and grew to 2,112 Billions by 1986.

The U.S. International Investment Position grew from 37 millions in the 1955 time period to 147 Billions in the 1982 time period and then decayed to a negative 60 Billions by the 1986 time period.

The U.S. Merchandise Trade Balance was 4.6 Billions positive in the 1960 time period and declined to 132 Billions negative by the 1985 time period.

The Consumer Price Index (CPI) was at a level of 0.88 in the 1955 time period and grew to 3.25 by the 1985 time period.

The Percentage Change in CPI grew from 1.5 per cent in the 1960 time period to 13.5 in the 1980 time period and reduced to 3.6 by the 1985 time period.

The Gross National Product (GNP) In Constant 1970 Dollars grew from 1,086 billions in the 1970 time period to 1,639 billions by the 1985 time period.

These data are presented to show how the "time period" does not accurately present the data in the proper way to allow one to reach conclusions about the critical events that caused the serious consequences. Several critical events have had significant effects on the total economic performance of the United States over the years.

Prior to the passage of the Tax Reform Act of 1969, the United States was the most powerful country in the world economically, militarily, and politically. The U.S. had a positive merchandise trade balance, a balanced Federal budget, and was the most productive country in the world. The tax law of 1954 had created the most positive investment climate that prevailed from 1960 to 1969—for those nine years real GNP grew at a compound rate of 4.335 per cent per year, unemployment was at 3 per cent, inflation was at 1.779 per cent per year, and there was a 3.25 Billion dollar surplus in 1969. The critical event that caused the significant decline of the United States was the Tax reform Act of 1969. Almost no economists seem to realize that that critical event was as important as it has been in causing the decline of our country. The data presented above certainly shows how the country has suffered but the presentation of the data does not point to the critical events that caused the decline. Tax law changes in 1976 and those of 1984 and 1986 have taken their toll in ruining the personal private investment climate in the United States. The country has been suffering ever since these tax laws were passed. Imagine deficits of hundreds of billions of dollars and a Federal Debt of $5 trillion!

CHAPTER NINE

# Some Very Important People Really Did Care

### *Some Did Care*

Senator Robert W. Kasten, Jr. in a May 1989 article in CFO magazine entitled, "Let's Sharpen America's Competitive edge—By Cutting the Capital Gains Tax,"[8] made an attempt to change the way we tax long term capital gains. His article showed that he really did care about the future of America.

Senator Kasten pointed out that one of America's worst competitive handicaps is purely self-inflicted: We impose the heaviest tax on capital gains in the free world. This tax cripples U.S. savings and investment—and without investment, new products and new technologies aren't developed, new plants aren't built, and new American jobs aren't created.

He further pointed out that many countries don't tax capital gains at all, and that the countries that do, tax such gains at much lower rates than the United States. Such policies reduce the cost of capital and in Japan, for example the cost of capital is 50 to 75 per cent lower than the cost in the U.S. The Senator teamed with President Bush to make capital gains reform proposals that would encourage the kind of investment that is essential for America's competitiveness. Such proposals would cut the capital gains rate in half, and limit the tax break to equities—that kind of investment sparks job creation, technological innovation, and small business formation. His proposals would exclude investments in collectibles and depreciable real property.

Senator Kasten's bill went further than the President by cutting the corporate capital gains rate in half, and indexing capital gains for any year that inflation exceeded 4 per cent. Such indexing would lower the tax burden on holders of non-equity assets, whose capital gains are due mostly to inflation. He contended that taxing investors on purely inflationary gain is fundamentally unjust.

He pointed out that when the rate of tax on capital gains was reduced in 1978, taxes paid on capital gains increased from 9.1 billion to 12.5 billion in 1980, and when the rate was cut further in 1981, to 20 per cent such taxes increased from 12.7 billion in 1981 to 24.5 billion in 1985.

Senator Kasten, a Republican from Wisconsin was a member of the Senate Budget Committee and concluded that other countries have adopted policies that reward saving, investing, and taking risk. Keeping our capital gains tax as high as it is amounts to a give-away of American jobs to our foreign competitors. We can sharpen America's competitive edge by bringing our capital gains rate in line with the rest of the world.

Senator Kasten and the President were only a voice in the wind against the views of Senator George Mitchell who established the Democratic Manifesto that cutting the capital gains tax was a **give-away to the rich!** Senator Mitchell was one of the horrible leaders of our country that really didn't care, one who was more interested in getting reelected than solving the terrible problems of high Federal Deficits and the unbelievable Federal Debt, not to mention problems of our negative trade balances, and lowered international competitiveness. Certainly he and many others like him didn't care.

## *Another Who Cared*

Walter H. Judd was a Congressman for 20 years. In the February 1976 Readers's Digest his article was titled, "Everyone Wants Economy—Without the Me!"[9] In that article, Mr. Judd quotes President Gerald Ford who addressed a joint session of Congress, and turned to House Speaker Carl Albert of Oklahoma. "Mr. Speaker I am a little late getting around to it, but confession is good for the soul. I have sometimes voted to spend taxpayers' money for worthy federal projects in Grand Rapids while I vigorously opposed wasteful spending boondoggles in Oklahoma."

Mr. Judd confided that in his years of public life he learned that politicians and citizens alike invariably claim that government spending must be restrained—except where the restraints cut off federal dollars flowing into their cities, their businesses, or their pocketbooks.

He claimed that legislators take inconsistent positions because the voters back home demand it, and cited an example: when he represented a Minneapolis district in Congress, a Republican businessman who normally decried deficit spending berated me for voting against a bill which would have brought several million dollars into our city. Judd answered with, "Where do you think federal funds for Minneapolis come from? People in St. Paul?

Mr. Judd wrote that legislators who yield to these pressures are responsible for the fact that federal spending is out of control. He added that it was 1962 when the federal budget exceeded $100 billion, in only nine years by 1971 it had passed $200 billion, and only four years later in 1975 it was over $300 billion.

What was more astounding was that the avalanche of spending was proceeding without regard to revenues. Federal Deficits in 15 of the last 17 years fueled inflation, so that the 1947 dollar was only worth 45 cents. Judd forecast that if the trend continued the dollar would be worth no more than a nickel.

Judd also presented some of the special-interest groups: The National Education Association wanted a program that would cost $60 billion a year. The American Association of Retired Persons want a program costing $7 billion a year. The AFL-CIO want a public service employment program and more public works costing $21 billion. The National League of Cities want increased revenue sharing, a public job program, expanded urban renewal, and U.S. aid for communities with high unemployment. Cost $12 billion.

Judd later stated, "... The fight for reasonable federal spending can be won only if all segments of our society curb their demands on government." Alexander Tyler warned, "A democracy cannot exist as a permanent form of government. It can only exist until the voters discover they can vote themselves largess out of the public treasury. From that moment on, the majority always votes for the candidate promising the most benefits from the public treasury—with the result that democracy collapses over a loose fiscal policy, always to be followed by a dictatorship."

## *Yet Another Who Cared*

One of my very good friends, an outstanding aeronautical engineer, who also was an outstanding doctor of medicine, and one of the clearest thinkers I have ever known, who could take the most complex problems and simplify them to arrive at a fine solution, reacted to the Senate vote to turn down the balanced budget amendment.

He wrote a letter to the Senate and complained about their rejection of the constitutional amendment to force the Congress to face their responsibilities that each year they insure that the federal budget was in balance or preferably in surplus so that our horrendous Federal Debt could eventually be reduced and eventually paid off.

He wrote, "Shame! Shame! Shame! Shame on the Senators who voted against the balanced budget amendment. Shame on the President who not only did not support the amendment, but actively used the influence of his office to persuade certain Democrats to vote against it. And Shame on the voters who have, year after year, elected a Congress that has shown no fiscal responsibility for at least the past 50 years with the end result of a Federal Debt approaching

5 trillion dollars. If a 5 trillion dollar debt isn't fiscal irresponsibility, I would like to know what is!

"Efforts to control Federal spending, some of which have actually resulted in legislation passed by the Congress (e.g., the Gramm-Rudman Bill) have failed because the Congress will not adhere to its own regulations.

"In my opinion it is an international disgrace that the United States has had to resort to proposing a constitutional amendment to assure that the Congress and the President will not be able to shirk their responsibilities any longer!

"There are those (Senator Feinstein and others) who say they would have voted for the amendment if it had contained the provision that Social Security would not be jeopardized by balancing the budget. As far as I am concerned, this is a red herring! The Constitution tells us what is to be done, NOT how to do it! It is the responsibility of the Congress and the President to implement compliance with the Constitution!

"Because two-thirds of the States must approve an amendment, the Senate has, in essence, denied the States an opportunity to vote. It is at the state level that arguments such as those of Senators Feinstein, Byrd, et al should be addressed.

"But, perhaps, because of human nature, this is an exercise in futility. Almost twenty years ago an article in the Reader's Digest by Congressman Walter M. Judd quoted a British historian." **And you have already seen that quote.**

"In the United States this prophesy has been right on the mark, especially over the last half century. Unless we not only have a balanced budget amendment, but also start a program of paying off the Federal Debt, the rest of this prophesy could become a reality!"

Concerned individuals like my friend Dr. Curtis E. Miller are people who care. It is going to take a lot of people who care to change our national policies to insure that people will invest in the future of the country, to create real economic growth, to improve our competitive position in world markets, to provide the wealth and revenues to pay our bills and eventually to pay off our horrendous federal debt, and to provide jobs for an ever growing population. The United States needs more investment by its people.

## *Even the Chinese Care*

The once totally communistic country of China has realized that it is important to care. The government leaders realized that what was needed was investment to provide the people with a higher standard of living. Austerity programs had been tried and had been found wanting. Although maintaining their government structure, they provided incentives to investment, and encouraged people to save and invest, not only their own people but they attracted outside investors. The result has been the economic growth at a rate of 12.8 per cent in 1992. Over a 13 year span their real economic growth rate has averaged over 9.0 per cent—and this compares to about 2 to 3 per cent for the United States. Imagine a country with close to one billion population growing at a rate more than three times that of the United States!

In a country that only fifteen years ago could barely provide food and shelter for its people, now those people are able to buy cosmetics and clothes that were unheard of years ago. There is no question that the standard of living in china has improved. One of the most telling statistics is the national savings rate of China. Over a fifteen year period the total savings rate in the United States was only one-third that of the Chinese. With such a high savings rate there is no question that eventually China will grow into a significant world economic power.

When communism was prevalent, the national budget reached as high as 50 per cent of the gross national product. Since the trend toward motivating people to save and invest, the national budget has fallen to 20 per cent of the gross national product. The result is that all the people have more of everything they need and now can spend their increased income for consumer products that were unthought-of under the old communist regime.

There is a lesson to be learned in the spectacular rise of China as a world economic power. Policies that foster saving and investment increase the standard of living for all people, and allow the economy to grow and grow.

While China, still a non-democratic country, has seen the power of investment and is nurturing and encouraging investment not only by its own people but also by outside enterprises, they are going in the right direction with their policies.

Here in the United States our Congress continues to ignore the lessons of history; the 1954 tax law created the very best investment climate provided over a fifteen year period. Personal investors grew from around 4 per cent of the population to almost 16 per cent until the Tax Reform Act of 1969 caused a serious decline in the investment climate, and investors shunned the New York Stock Exchange, by pulling over 100 billion dollars out of the market. New companies that needed equity capital to create jobs, and to develop new technologies slid from over 649 in 1969 to 9 by 1976, since venture capital sources dried up because of the serious degradation of the investment climate as a result of the higher risk-to-reward ratio, when taxes were taken into account. Even more devastating was the drop in small technical companies seeking equity capital—200 such companies went to the market for added equity capital in 1969 but by 1976 only two small technical companies were able to raise equity capital. What a tragic result of tax policy. Such small companies create jobs at a rate of growth 60 times larger than that of large companies and this is supported by data from the U.S. Department of Labor.

## *A Congressman Who Cares*

Christopher Cox, chairman of the Republican Policy Committee, testified before the House Ways and Means Committee on June 7, 1995.[10] To emphasize how terribly complex the Internal Revenue Code has become he cited the time that he was on a television show with the then Commissioner of Internal Revenue. Cox asked, "Do you use an accountant to help you prepare your taxes?" Cox confessed that he did, even though he once taught tax law at Harvard. The Commissioner Fred Goldberg admitted that he, too, needed help to do his taxes.

Cox stated, "It's no wonder: the eight volumes of the Internal Revenue Code and Regulations now run more than 14,700 pages.

That's not counting another 200,000 pages of decisions and interpretations. Perhaps that is why our Founding Fathers prevented against an income tax in the Constitution. It took the 16th Amendment in 1913 to permit one. Yet even the amendment's sponsors would be horrified to see what the income tax has become: the most invasive and hated interference of the federal government in the lives of ordinary citizens."

The chief Republican sponsor of the 16th amendment, Rep. Sereno Payne of New York, supported it only because he believed that the country should have the option of taxing income in time of war.

Cox further said, "As to the general policy of the income tax, I am opposed to it. I believe, with Gladstone, that it tends to make a nation of liars ... it is in a word, a tax upon the income of honest men and an exemption, to a greater or lesser extent, of the income of rascals."

The leading Democratic sponsor, Minority Leader Champ Clark of Missouri offered his support for the amendment in the context of the income tax bill that was then being debated. The bill contained a $5,000 exemption, meaning that nobody who earned this amount paid any income tax at all. Cox adjusted these figures for inflation, and repeated Clark's remarks made on the floor of the House when he was arguing for the bill:

"I do not believe that the $82,000 is too much ... I certainly would increase it rather than diminish it, and for this reason: $82,000 is not an unreasonable amount for a man to support a family on and educate his children; $99,000 would not be an unreasonable amount; $115,000 would not be an unreasonable amount. But I say that when a man's net income rises above $1.65 million a year, it does not make any difference to him, practically, whether you take 1%, 2%, 5%, or 25%.

Cox further stated, "It is easy to see why the income tax law was passed: Everyone believed that someone else would pay. As recently as the eve of Pearl Harbor, only one in seven Americans was even required to file an income tax return. The last time we had a Republican Congress, in 1954, the federal tax burden on the average American family was one-tenth of what it is today.

"But today, if you're like most people, you pay several hundred per cent more in income taxes than your parents did. More than 95% of all taxpayers who are forced to file income tax returns are people who were promised by the sponsors of the 16th Amendment that they would never be taxed at all.

"Because of the twin evils of the income tax and the endlessly expanding welfare state, middle America now bears a much greater government burden than when I was a child. In the 1950's, government did not consume the 40% of our gross domestic product it does today, but half that. As a result, the average American family, making the average national income (then), paid an income tax rate of just 2%."

Cox continued, "That average family of my parents' generation could afford a three-bedroom home, even though the norm was that only one spouse had to work. They paid only 4% interest on their 30 year mortgage. Their FICA payroll taxes were just 1.5%. All of this was possible because the federal budget was balanced in a low-tax environment.

"That kind of freedom and opportunity is again possible. But it will become reality only if we are actually willing to reduce the size of government, and only if we recognize that the income tax is an experiment that has failed miserably.

"On July 12, 1909 Rep. Samuel McCall of Massachusetts looked into the future and asked a troubling question about the 16th Amendment, which the House approved later that day:

"Why drag every government power to Washington so that a vast, centralized government may devour the states and the liberty of individuals as well? I say this amendment should be more carefully considered than it has yet been considered.'

"In the intervening decades, the American people have had ample opportunity to consider the income tax, and they have found it sorely wanting. It has become exactly what McCall feared. It deserves to die."

Cox is certainly correct in concluding that the Internal Revenue Code is far too complex to be understandable to most individuals, in fact, it is too complex to be administered by agents of the Internal Revenue Service, leading to continuing controversy between able and competent agents and the individuals subject to question or audit. Imagine an individual having to be familiar with 14,700 pages of the Code and also with 200,000 pages of decisions and interpretations.

The author has had the experience of having an agent refer to the wrong section of the Code and tell him that such an activity was not correct, yet when the author objected, and pointed to the correct section of the Code, the agent remarked, "How come you know so much about the Code?" The author's response was, "I have to protect myself from agents like you."

The terrible result of the confusion caused by the complexity of the Internal Revenue Code, in its effect on individuals, is that there is uncertainty leading to resistance by individuals to make the critical decision to invest rather than to consume, a decision that has tremendous effect on the economic health of the nation's economy.

When individuals decide to invest good things happen: new products and new technology are developed, real economic growth increases, new jobs are created, productivity improves, tax revenues increase, and the competitiveness in world markets rises, all of this helps to make possible the creation of Federal surpluses, and eventually reductions in the nation's horrendous debt.

Christopher Cox is to be commended for taking the time to study the history of the 16th Amendment, and subsequent changes in the laws relating to the taxation of the nation's individuals. Our tax laws are truly in a state of chaos!

## *Another Who Really Cared*

Malcolm Wallop a former rancher, businessman, Army officer, state legislator of Big Horn Wyoming was elected to the United States Senate in 1976, 1982, and 1988, retired from public office in January of 1995. Wallop was chairman of the Republican Senate Steering Committee, minority leader of the Senate Committee on Energy and Natural Resources, member of the Select Committee on Intelligence, member of the Senate Committee on Finance, Armed

Services, Judiciary, the Environment, Public Works, and Small Business.

Certainly here is a man with outstanding background in the political arena, who really tried to get something done to improve the posture of the United States in the world scene. He strongly believed that the nation was going in the wrong direction, and stated, "America is in danger of becoming a nation of favor-seekers and dependents. Her political leaders as well as her ordinary citizens must recover their once widely shared and deep commitment to personal responsibility and independence."

Wallop stated, "Today government touches almost everything in America and harms almost everything it touches. Federal, state, and local governments together spend 42 out of every 100 dollars we earn. Those who do the taxing and spending have long since ceased to work for the people as a whole. Rather, they work for themselves and for their clients—the education industry, the welfare culture, public-employee unions, etc. Most Americans sense that our ever rising taxes are feeding a machine hostile to our values. They ask, "Who represents us? Who is on our side?" Continuing, "Liberal government employees hire their own kind, and fund hundreds of advocacy groups, endowments for the arts and humanities, and their own radio and television net work."

Wallop asked, "Will we go the way of Argentina? Sixty years ago, Argentina was second only to the United States in per-capita wealth. Then its middle class listened to Juan Peron's siren song of entitlements. Taxes, regulations, and interest-group power soon reduced the country to genteel poverty, then to grinding poverty and food riots. Now it has changed course—it is even privatizing social security. We meanwhile are heading where Argentina was, pulled along by Hillary Clinton's imitation of Eva Peron."

Wallop believes that the "flat tax" would be a good thing for the country and "would avoid the present hypocrisy of nominal taxes indexed upward, while taxes after loopholes are actually indexed downward."

The ex-Senator really believes in America, and is trying to do something to change our course. He wants to end the tyranny of the federal over state and local governments, to restore personal responsibility, to privatize rather than socialize medicine, to restore control of education to parents, and to allow communities to set their own moral standards. As correct as the man is in many of his ideas and proposals his advocation of the flat tax indicates a lack of understanding of the importance of motivating individuals to invest rather to consume. The differential tax rate for people who have the courage to invest and take a risk, and thereby to defer consumption of the nation's wealth, and to increase the supply of products and services, is essential to creating the pressure on individuals to invest.

Ex-Senator Wallop is a man who cares, and we should support him in his new endeavors: The Frontiers of Freedom Foundation, and the Conservative Television Network (CTN). Men like him need our encouragement and support.

## *One Democrat and One Republican Really Did Care*

Orrin Hatch Republican Senator from Utah and Joseph Lieberman Democratic Representative from Connecticut joined together to sponsor The Capital Formation Act and described it briefly in the Los Angeles Times issue of August 22, 1995.[11]

"Ever since the 1986 Tax Reform Act hiked capital gains taxes for most Americans, pundits and politicians have been debating how the Federal government should tax people who save and invest. While many have expressed sincere concerns over who would benefit, a few members of the old class-warfare school have spread a number of myths about how capital gets created in this country and who benefits from its creation.

"While the two of us have had our differences, we agree on what it takes to guarantee capital creation and thus job growth. Our Capital Formation Act embodies these beliefs. It provides a 50% exclusion from taxation on gains from capital assets, effectively lowering the top rate from 28% to 19.8%. Then building on the President's 1993 capital gains initiatives, it excludes an additional 25% of the long term gains from investment in a qualified small business or allows the investor to roll over a gain from one qualified small business into another and defer the gain altogether. This approach dispels the myths that anti-growth opponents have used to cloud the issue.

"The first myth is that capital gains needs to be a class issue, giving benefits to the wealthy while leaving the poor to hold the bag. Our bill explicitly provides the greatest tax rate reduction to lower and middle-income taxpayers. These Americans, with taxable incomes less than $40,000 per year, will only have to pay a 7.5% tax on their capital gains. Single digit tax rates would again be a reality for many Americans.

"Of course most capital gains are earned by Americans with higher incomes. The second myth we keep hearing is that the benefits of any capital gains relief will go to the 'top 1%.' But these 'high-income' Americans include anyone who realizes a gain on the sale of a home or small business. We have heard from countless middle-income constituents who are stunned to find that simply selling a home, farm, or small business makes them, for one year, a part of the fabled 'top 1%' the growth-o-phobes so often mention.

"The third myth is that capital gains must necessarily be partisan. On this point, a little history: In 1992 50 Democrats in the Senate and 209 in the House voted for a broad-based cut in capital gains taxation. Just as dramatically, the 1993 Democratic budget package provided a 50% capital gains exclusion for qualified small businesses.

"When President Clinton's 1993 capital gains tax cut clearly created opportunities for Americans of wealth, we heard no class-warfare outcry. Members on both sides of the aisle recognized that the way to create jobs is to create opportunity, and the way to create opportunity is to not tax it out of existence.

"By building on pro-investment policies from both parties, combining broad-based capital gains relief for all Americans with a targeted exclusion for what House Speaker Newt Gingrich refers to as 'baby businesses'—tomorrow's high-growth firms—we are taking an important step toward the job-creating economy of the next century."

These gentlemen should be lauded for their bi-partisan approach to solving our country's most pressing problem—the lack of investment to create jobs, to improve productivity, to drive economic growth, and eventually to provide the tax revenues to balance the nation's budget.

## *This Senator Certainly Cares*

In the Summer of 1995 Senator Connie Mack had an article in the Wall Street Journal, "Capital Gains Taxes—A $1.5 Trillion Opportunity."[12] In it he made some outstanding points.

Mack wrote that the Dow Jones Industrial Average had soared 185% over the past nine years, as new markets, products, and technologies have boosted the earnings potential of the U.S. economy. In spite of this, capital gains revenues had stagnated. He asked, "Why?" And he blamed it on the high capital gains tax rates.

The Senator contended that the slow-down was directly related to the misguided 1986 increase in the capital gains tax rate. He wrote, "The capital gains tax is locking investors into old investments, and is pushing investors into tax-free investments such as pension funds, 401(k)s, individual retirement accounts and trusts. In all, economists at the Joint Economic Committee estimate $1.5 trillion in capital gains are locked up in the economy, awaiting a reduction in the capital gains tax rate."

Mack stated that the real capital gains tax rate, even at very low levels of inflation, can be higher than 100%, because taxes are levied on both real gains and the illusory gains due to inflation. He also pointed out that many foreign countries with lower capital gains taxes offer a more inviting climate for investment, while U.S. companies must take drastic steps to insure a great enough return on equity investment to attract capital. Those drastic steps result in cuts in payroll and expenses. At the same time new industry, which tends to add most new jobs in the economy, must fight for capital and pay more for it.

"Cutting the capital gains tax rate and indexing it for inflation are clear ways to boost economic growth, job creation—and government revenues. At a time when Congress is getting serious about balancing the budget, cutting the capital gains tax rate has the potential to boost Federal revenues by more than $225 billion (assuming $1.5 trillion in capital gains taxed at a 20% rate, adjusting for offsetting losses). That amounts to seven years of capital gains tax revenue at the current pace." He also pointed out that this estimate of revenue gains is related only to capital gains and does not take into account the increase in real economic growth from a cut in the capital gains tax rate.

Discussing the broader impact of cutting the capital gains tax rate, He stated, "Because capital gains result only from the sale of an asset, and investors decide when to sell, that makes the capital gains tax a voluntary tax. Granted, investors make decisions based on many different inputs. However, historical data on capital gains realizations show that tax rates are a significant factor. After the capital gains tax rate was cut to 20% in 1982, capital gains realizations during the four years from 1983 to 1986 totaled $763 billion, more than double the $369.3 billion in realizations in the previous five years.

"Part Of this dramatic gain was due to a surge in 1986, when capital gains realizations shot up 90.6% as investors took gains before tax rates went up in 1987 from an effective top rate of 20% to 28%. Since 1987, capital gains realizations have fallen back to levels 35% below those of the three years before the capital gains tax increase. This decline in realizations has occurred despite record-setting gains in the stock market."

Lamenting the negative effects of the 1986 increase in the capital gains tax, Mack observes, "In effect, we threw away the key to investment and economic growth in 1987 when the capital gains tax rate was increased. Between 1985 and 1994, the S&P 500 increased 146%. If capital gains realizations had kept pace with the S&P 500, there would have been $2.7 trillion in realizations between 1987 and 1994. Instead, using any reasonable estimate of actual realizations for 1994, there was less than $1.2 trillion. This suggests that at least $1.5 trillion is locked-up or forced into inflexible tax-free investment strategies. Obviously, investors are refusing to sell in the face of punitive tax treatment. The nearby chart shows the shortfall in capital gains realizations suggested by the stock market gains. (These estimates used 1985 realizations as a base, so that the artificial boost in 1986 did not lead to an overstatement of potential gains.)

Mack further observes, "It's true that 'hot' new companies are attracting capital regardless of the current tax system. Nevertheless, despite the tremendous rise in the stock market during recent years, total investment of venture capital in companies remains below 1986 levels. According to Securities Data Co., venture-backed company investment in 1994 was $2.7 billion, only $60 million higher than in 1985 and $501 million below 1986. And, while initial public offerings have increased as the stock market reaches new highs, the 1994 IPO total of 646 is still below the 728 in 1986."

Mack correctly states the importance of the capital gains tax rate upon the country's future, "Entrepreneurial talent requires resources, and the opportunities today are the greatest they have been in decades. New technology is opening the door to productivity gains and a potential for new products not seen since the Industrial Revolution. By reducing the capital gains tax rate and indexing it for inflation, the $1.5 trillion in locked-up gains can be released to pursue investment opportunities that create jobs and growth in the U.S. economy."

Having a man such as Senator Mack as chairman of the Joint Economic Committee is a truly positive development in our legislative activity for the future. What a striking contrast his knowledge and understanding of the effects of the tax laws upon the future of our country when compared with the totally false and misguided opinions and beliefs of Joseph J. Minarik, Executive Director for Policy and Chief Economist, House of Representatives Committee on the Budget. We need to support knowledgeable and capable men like Connie Mack and we need to rid our total legislative system of ignorant, misguided, and dangerous men in positions of power and important advisory posts. It is no wonder we are in serious trouble when men like Mack are ignored and men like Minarik are in positions of power and have the ears of legislators.

Why is it that legislators cannot screen applicants for positions like Chief Economist, and Director of Policy for such important posts in the legislative halls of our country? Such a biased and incorrect set of opinions should certainly become obvious to discerning personnel executives of the legislative body who should be instrumental in the hiring of experts to assist the Congressional committees to carry out their critical responsibilities. Ideology rather than competence seems to be more important than knowledge, experience, and wisdom. Some of the appointees seem to be completely devoid of understanding and knowledge of history—apparently their personal biases are more important than their objectivity—in solving the nation's problems of continuing federal deficits, unemployment, lack of real economic growth, negative international trade balances, lagging productivity increases, and high interest rates. Certainly the advice given by many economists working for the Congress have led to the horrendous federal debt resulting from continuing federal deficits, and loss of our position as the world's diplomatic, economic, and military leader. We need powerful remedies now—we must completely discredit the advisors who have led the nation to its sorry current posture in the world. We can revitalize America, we must do it now!

## *Even Some Governors Care*

In December 1994 the Wall Street Journal contained a small item by one of its staff reporters:

> BOSTON—Massachusetts Gov. William Weld signed into law a bill that would eliminate the capital gains tax for assets held for at least six years.
>
> Current law taxes capital gains at 12% for assets held for less than one year, and at 6% thereafter. Under the new law, an asset held for three years would incur a capital gains tax of 3%, but nothing for assets held for at least six years.
>
> Gov. Weld said the change will encourage investment and stimulate the state's economy. "Cutting capital gains in this manner will ensure that homeowners and other patient investors are no longer taxed for taking a risk, or whacked by the effect of inflation."

> As part of his tax package, Gov. Weld also signed into law tax cuts for lower income families.

This action by Governor Weld shows that there are some people in the country who understand the value of motivating individuals to invest in the future of their country. Also there are some people who realize that investment brings with it some element of risk and should be treated differently than income generated without taking any risk. Those same people also realize that when one invests he is also creating opportunities to create new products, new technology, improvements in productivity, increases in economic growth, and thereby increases in Federal tax revenues.

Imagine the investor who resided in Massachusetts who must pay a 28% tax on his capital gain to the Federal Internal Revenue Service and 12% of his capital gain to the State of Massachusetts. For example let us assume a long term capital gain of $10,000: Before the recent change in the law $1,200 would be paid to the State, and $2,800 would be paid to the IRS. Let us assume further that the original cost of the asset was $5,000 and it was sold for $15,000. After taxes the value to the taxpayer would be $11,000, so that to regain the loss to taxes the taxpayer must re-invest the $11,000 at some new investment that would return at least a 36.36% higher return than the taxpayer would get from his prior investment. The critical decision which the taxpayer must make is whether such a higher return is possible with his new investment. If such a higher return is not possible, the taxpayer would not have sold his asset but would have been "locked in" to his original investment. As one can see not only does the new tax law improve the motivation to invest, but it also reduces the level of required higher rate of return to re-invest. As such the new law improves the mobility of capital from one investment to another.

The pressure of the tax law on investors is critical to making not only original investments but also is important to making the decision to change investments. A study of tax laws of other countries makes it clear that tax law has a tremendous effect on the investment climate of any country. The combination of the savings rate and the investment rate are important to the rate of growth of the economy. Tax policy is undeniably responsible for raising or lowering the savings rate and the investment rate in any country.

## *Merrill Lynch Really Cares*

In a May 1995 publication of "Legislative Update"[13] Merrill Lynch stated, "For some time now, Merrill Lynch has been urging Washington policy makers to take steps to increase saving and encourage investment."

"We have consistently asked the White House and members of Congress to consider that Washington has an opportunity—in fact, a responsibility—to help solve the saving crisis in America.

The personal monthly saving rate has fallen from about 8% of disposable income in the late 1960's to as low as 4% recently, a drop that harms economic growth and deprives the U.S. economy of billions of dollars in investment capital. The low level of saving also makes the American Dream much more difficult to achieve, posing a serious threat to the future financial security of millions of Americans.

Today, baby boomers (Americans between the ages of 30 and 48) are saving at only one-third the rate needed for a secure retirement. Half of all American families now have less than $1,000 in net financial assets—far too little for any kind of financial security.

Fortunately, Congress is now giving serious consideration to measures that would encourage saving and investment. The House of Representatives recently passed a major tax reduction bill, with additional provisions promoting saving. The Senate is now considering that legislation.

Those provisions include:

- A new individual retirement account, the American Dream Savings Account, that would allow individuals to make non-deductible contributions of up to $2,000 a year ($4,000 for couples). After five years, tax-and penalty free withdrawals would be permitted for a number of specified purposes, including retirement, first home purchases, college costs, and significant medical expenses.

- A deductible contribution to an IRA of up to $2,000 per year for non-working spouses.
- A reduction in the capital gains tax, providing a 50% exclusion of capital gains income. (This would, for example, reduce the top effective tax rate for a taxpayer to 19.8% in the highest bracket.) The bill would also index capital gains for assets acquired after Dec. 31, 1994, and held for more than three years.

These and other provisions will be the subject of much debate in the U.S. Senate this summer. We will keep you informed as the bill makes its way through the legislative process."

All Americans should support Merrill Lynch in their endeavor to get this bill passed. All Americans would benefit from the provisions contained in this bill. Saving our country from economic chaos is the reason for this book. We have got to have legislation such as this to increase the availability of capital to invest to create jobs, to fight inflation, to improve productivity, to increase economic growth, to drive interest rates down, to improve our international trade balances, and eventually to provide the necessary revenues to balance the Federal budget, and eventually to reduce the horrendous Federal Debt.

## *Some People Tried to Help*

In a July 25, 1969 issue of a publication by Loeb, Rhoades & Co., of their Fortnightly Review an article entitled, "About ways and Means,"[14] their author discusses the purposes of a sane tax policy: to provide necessary revenues for government, and to correct social injustices. In discussing the activities of the Ways and Means Committee of the House of Representatives they believed that the current activities served neither purpose. Those activities threatened to diminish the incentives to save as well as the liquidity of capital markets.

The author stated that income from the sale of assets has been subject to preferentially low tax rates ever since 1921. The rate of tax on capital gains has been only 50 per cent of the tax on ordinary income. At the time the Committee was considering raising the rate of tax on capital gains, and the author was motivated to recall why capital gains are differentiated from ordinary income in the first place. Any change in that policy should be clearly understood before tinkering with existing provisions on this subject.

"Investment gains are to some extent illusory rather than real," he stated, "a fact of which one need not be reminded in a period of inflation. Investment gains are possible only by venturing one's savings, the fruits of earlier earnings on which taxes have already been paid."

Pointing out that the success of our capitalistic system has been built on adequate incentives, not only for making a decent living, but also for building up savings and investments. He also observed that the proposed changes would lead to an extension of the locking-in process, to decreased liquidity of financial markets, and to a diminution of the availability of venture capital.

Here the author was right on target, since, when the Congress passed the 1969 Tax Reform Act, venture capital dried up as pointed out elsewhere in this book.

The author also pointed out the erroneous calculations made by the Joint Internal Revenue Committee staff provided to the Ways and Means Committee that there would be an annual revenue gain of $715 million if the 25 per cent alternative tax rate on capital gains were eliminated. (Actually there was a significant decrease in capital gains tax revenues after the 1969 law became effective.)

The author stated, "But the interest in a more careful consideration of tax reform than is possible in an overheated atmosphere does extend well beyond the ranks of 26 million shareholders here and abroad; it extends to all who care for the preservation of adequate incentives within our free enterprise system and in a smoothly functioning process of saving and investing." Senator Russell B. Long had already said, "The Senate is gripped with tax reform fever." And the author felt that a feverish disposition is not the proper frame of mind to make lasting arrangements for a subsequent condition of vibrant health.

The predictions made in the article have come to pass: Inflation, unemployment, low economic growth, reduced growth in productivity, higher interest rates, all these factors of national performance were seriously degraded after the passage of the Tax Reform Act of 1969.

You must conclude that the author tried to influence the Congress to do the right thing, but his were cries in the wilderness, and completely ignored by the Congress. Is it that they didn't care?

## *Some People Cared about the Problem*

In a conference on economic policy on Friday and Saturday September 1 and 2, 1995 in Jackson, Wyoming,[15] a number of important people addressed the problem of continuing Federal Deficits. Some of the world's leading economists and economic policy-makers had some bad news for Republican congressional leaders: The GOP's plan to balance the budget over the next seven years will barely make a dent in America's long-term budget problems. Federal Reserve officials and other leaders largely agreed that the deficit-reduction proposals now being debated in Washington ignore the long-term problem of entitlement spending. What these so-called experts missed is that there has not been enough real economic growth of the U.S. economy over the last 25 years. And the reason for this lack of annual growth in gross national product has been the negative personal private investment climate. Growth in the economy inherently creates tax revenues without raising tax rates, and the increased revenues permit the country to balance its budget and eventually to reduce its burgeoning Federal Debt.

The consensus was that not only does Washington need to reduce the annual deficit, it must start running large surpluses over the next decade or two to avoid "the detonation of a fiscal time bomb when Social Security and Medicare run out of money as baby boomers retire."

Alan Auerbach, a former congressional staff member and now an economist at University of California Berkeley stated, "U.S. fiscal policy is far more unbalanced than the recent deficit figures suggest, even if taxes and spending are adjusted to achieve a balanced budget in the short run, changing demographics will still cause U.S. fiscal policy to be unsustainable."

June O'Neill, Congressional Budget Office Director said, "We shouldn't think that just because these future problems are so large that deficit reduction now is irrelevant."

The discussions made evident the degree to which officials of the Federal Reserve and other economists are baffled by the inability of the political system to address the looming entitlement crisis. What surprised the author was that no one seemed to recognize the importance of the lack of real economic growth as the central problem over the last 26 years.

Federal Reserve Board Chairman, Alan Greenspan pointed out, "We must stress that today's actions and commitments (to cut the deficit) are only the first step to fiscal reform that must be consolidated by future legislators, indeed, the will and the means to follow through are at least as important."

Auerbach further stressed, "The failure of past budget reforms to curb entitlements has skewed Federal spending increasingly toward fast-growing benefits for senior citizens. As a result the government has to begin running surpluses now to prepare for the time early in the 21st century when the trust funds for Medicare and Social Security are depleted and the overall Federal Deficit begins to balloon again."

Auerbach calculated that future generations will face the equivalent of an 84.4% lifetime rate of federal, state and local taxes, contrasted with the 34.2% faced by wage earners now. He said, "Those figures indicate just how infeasible it would be to exempt all existing generations from the burden."

Peter Peterson, chairman of the Blackstone Group, an investment banking firm and co-founder of the Concord Coalition, a bi-partisan economic policy group noted, "Indeed, entitlement costs are already frightening," and calculated that the entitlements that heavily serve the middle class, such as Social Security and Medicare, now equal 9.2% of the gross domestic product of the United States. The Federal government is spending $15,701 per capita on senior citizens, compared to just $1,253 per capita on children younger than 18.

What a nonsensical comparison! Most of the children younger than 18 are supported by their own parents—very few of the senior citizens are supported by their children!

There is no doubt that the Federal Reserve would be happy to see strong actions taken by Congress to reduce the Federal Deficit. It is agreed by economists at this meeting that if the President and the Congress impose long-term limits on entitlement spending and other Federal outlays, the Fed could begin to move to cut rates so that those budget cuts do not harm economic growth. Tough budget action by Congress would put greater political pressure on the Fed to pursue an easier monetary policy.

John Taylor, a Stanford University economist, once budget cuts are in place would, "recommend gradually reducing interest rates at roughly the same pace as the budget deficit actually declines." In his paper he contended, "A seven-year program to reduce the deficit would thus be accompanied by a seven-year monetary adjustment program with interest rates being adjusted each year."

Economists at the conference certainly were not unanimous in their opinions. Laurence Ball of Johns Hopkins University, and N. Gregory Mankiw of Harvard University in a paper presented at the conference contended, "the cumulative effects of past budget deficits on U.S. economic growth have been small, and estimated that the nation has lost a combined total of six percentage points of gross domestic product or about $400 Billion of economic output, as a result of past deficits. Thus reducing growth by **6%** is like giving up about three years of growth, in the absence of debt, the U.S. would have achieved its 1995 level of income in 1992. These numbers are certainly significant, but waiting three years to achieve any level of income is hardly any disaster."

What all these so-called experts argue about, indicates they really don't realize that the trouble with our country is the fouled up personal private investment climate. What they don't understand is that, if in the last 26 years, we had grown at a level of 4.335% per year rather than one or two per cent per year, we would have had an $850 billion surplus last year instead of a deficit. Why is it that economists don't seem to understand the power of personal, private investment in creating real economic growth for our country??

Not one of the experts discussed the personal private investment climate effects upon jobs, inflation, new products, new technology, real economic growth, and eventually the Federal Deficits, and ultimately the total Federal Debt. Why don't they understand? Perhaps because they have never created a new product, created a new job, developed a new technology, or taken a risk to make an investment to make such things happen. None of the experts discussed the effects of the country's tax policy upon the investment climate—the real cause of our long-term problems. High tax rates don't produce high revenues, high real economic growth rates do produce higher revenues and allow the country to balance its budgets and eventually to pay off some of its horrendous debt. Why don't they understand? Certainly the conference proves that they care and want to do something to help solve some of our country's problems.

## *Even Those Who Care Can Be Misled*

According to the Congressional Record of August 6, 1969,[16] Mr. Wilbur D. Mills opened floor debate on H.R. 13270 to reform the income tax laws. Mr. Mills stated, "This is the day I have looked forward to for a long time.

"I suppose I have been as concerned as anyone about the need for changes in the Internal Revenue Code over the years that I have been in the House. Actually this is not the first time that changes have been made. I would remind my colleagues who were here in 1958 of the pressures under which the Committee on Ways and Means and the House itself worked in the drafting and passage of legislation relating to the taxation of life insurance companies. Then again more of you will remember the work in 1961 that went into what became the Revenue Act of 1962. Again in 1963 there were many changes included in the Revenue Act of 1964. The reforms in those bills were extensive in nature. However, none of them—not even all of them combined—covered nearly as much, or were as broad in scope as the beneficial changes that are contained in the bill presently before the committee."

While Mr. Mills did understand that the changes were extensive, there was no way that he could predict the terrible consequences of the passage of this bill. Mr. Mills was one who really did care, but he was misled by faulty analysis of the effects of the bill.

Mr. Mills continued, "In the past I have not detected as much interest in change for improvement and for greater equity as I have detected in the last year or so. Why this great interest in tax reform developed within that time, I do not know. Perhaps the people who say that it was triggered by the enactment of the surcharge last year by this House are right, because then we did increase taxes by 10 percent for a temporary period."

While the bill did respond to the cries for "greater equity," no one seemed to be alert to the serious detrimental effects of the bill upon the personal private investment climate, an effect that would see inflation soar, continuing Federal Deficits, lack of growth in productivity and real economic growth, interest rates increase to as high as 16 per cent, and serious negative balances of international trade. In the five years after the passage of this bill that is exactly what happened.

While 1800 companies went to the market for equity capital in 1969, in the next five years only 150 companies were able to raise sorely needed equity capital. It was even worse for small companies. In 1969 649 small companies with less net worth than $5 million were able to raise new equity capital, but by 1976 only 9 were able to approach the market successfully. For small technical companies, 200 raised equity capital in 1969, yet by 1976 only 2 were able to raise sorely needed capital. These are economic facts not some hollow theory. This is history not conjecture.

Mr. Mills was under tremendous pressure from his constituents, and stated, "I have never noticed in the past on any matter such a volume of mail coming to the Ways and Means Committee office from all over the United States as I have observed entering that office in connection with the legislation now pending before the House." He is probably correct in assuming that the previous 10 per cent increase in EVERYONE'S tax bill got a lot of constituents' attention. Certainly many people responded to the unhidable, real tax increase that hit everyone, not just a few. It got their attention!

Mr. Mills further states, "There is no doubt in my mind that when any of these preferences were written into the law, there was a reason for doing so. Let me tell you about one case that provides a good example on this point. In the late 1920's—and I know there were two members here then that are here now, and maybe there are others—a man in Philadelphia died possessed of a great estate. In the process of dividing it among his children, he left a very sizable amount of money to a daughter who had become a Catholic nun pledged by her vows not to have income nor to own property.

"The property passed to her in a trust in a form which made it impossible for her to divest herself of the property. As a result the law was changed in order to permit her to give all of the income from this property to the church.

"So we passed a provision that became known as the unlimited charitable contribution provision, for her benefit. I am satisfied that there is not a man or lady on the floor of the House today, who would not have voted for that proposition, faced with the argument that was then made by the Committee on Ways and Means for this very fine lady.

"But do you realize that this provision in 1966 enabled 49 people who have qualified for the unlimited charitable contribution year after year to avoid payment of all taxes on incomes which ranged from $200,000 to over $16,000,000."

The horrible example shocked the nation when former Treasury Secretary Joe Barr said that 154 high income people with incomes as high as $200,000 per year and more had avoided payment of all income taxes. But Joe Barr never told the people that 49 of those 154 had elected to give away all of their income to charities, and universities. Imagine 105 people out of 80 million taxpayers were able to take advantage of provisions of the law and not pay any income taxes—that is 1.313 per million people—so what? So we burn down the house to catch a few rats? And in the process cause our country to lose its leadership position in the world's economy.

Mr. Mills was guilty of some fallacious reasoning in his remarks. He stated, "These people make charitable contributions, I am certain, with the very highest of philanthropic motives. But at the same time they receive substantial tax advantages because they usually give away assets that have been in their family for a long time. For example, an asset which initially may have cost $10 but today may be valued at $100. In this case they receive a charitable deduction at today's market value of $100 for something that actually cost $10.

They can, for example, give away stocks in their portfolio that have appreciated in value and then with this year's earnings buy back at today's market price the same stocks—and the same identical number of shares."

Let's understand how fallacious this little example of false reasoning is. For example, you own $1 million of market value of IBM stock. Your taxable income is $1 million. You give away the $1 million of IBM to Stanford University. You've earned $1 million of taxable income and your estate has the same value as if you had earned nothing, if as Mr. Mills suggests you use your earnings to buy $1 million of IBM stock at today's market price.

If you did nothing your estate would have grown from $1 million by as much as $329,010 to $1,329,010. The government would have collected $670,980 in taxes and Stanford would have $1 million less in their endowment. Stanford loses and the government wins, But the taxpayer is $329,010 better off if he doesn't give anything away.

The taxpayer has suffered a loss of $329,010 to his estate as a result of making the gift to Stanford, but Stanford has benefited to the extent of $1 million. From a social standpoint will society be better off if Stanford has an additional $1 million, the taxpayer loses $329,010, and the government gets no benefit? Or will society be better off if the government gets $670,890, Stanford gets nothing and the taxpayers estate increases its value by $329,010?

Certainly there are social impacts from the tax policies of our Internal Revenue Code. Who is to judge the relative benefits to society, when the taxpayer makes a decision either to give or not to give? The Congress phased out the unlimited charitable contribution provision over a five year period. Bully for them! No doubt universities have suffered and churches have suffered and other important charitable institutions have suffered—and is the country better off as a result of this change in the tax code?

While there are social implications of many elements of the tax code, there are much more important economic implications of the provisions of the tax code. The important conclusion to be reached is IT IS NOT THAT THE GOVERNMENT TAXES ITS CITIZENS, BUT THE **WAY** THAT THE GOVERNMENT TAXES ITS CITIZENS!

If the tax code provisions motivate the citizens to consume rather than invest, citizens will consume rather than invest. If interest, dividends, and capital gains are taxed heavily, there is less pressure on the citizens to invest.

Mr. Mills gave a number of cases where taxpayers were able to avoid taxes and one of these he stated, "In our examination of these cases, I believe I have already said we found that there were 49 with unlimited charitable contribution deductions. In many of these cases, the cost was little if anything to the taxpayer because the contributions were composed largely of appreciation in the value of assets which never had been taxed."

Again let's examine the effect on the taxpayer if he gives, and the effect if he doesn't give as in the previous example. Let's assume that the taxpayer has $1 million in IBM stock which cost him $300,000. If he sold the stock he would have an estate of:

1,000,000 – 175,000 = 825,000

If he paid income tax on $1 million of income he would net:

1,000,000 – 670,890 = 329,010

Now his estate would be worth $1,154,010.

If he gave 1 million to charity he would pay no income tax and his estate would have a value of 1 million. The giving has cost the taxpayer $154,010. To assume that the gift cost the taxpayer nothing is erroneous. If the taxpayer's social decision is to give for the good of the country it certainly does cost him a significant amount of his net worth. But that is his choice. If the taxpayer believes Stanford can do more good for the country with $1 million than the United States can with $670,890 in tax revenue, he will probably give. If he is more interested in the growth of his own estate, he should not give but should pay his taxes and see his net worth grow. Again this is a social decision, there are much more important considerations when contemplating changes in tax policy. The most important considerations should be the economic strength of our country.

**"Illusion is the First of all pleasures,"** Voltaire.

A truly great Senator, the Honorable Russell B. Long who was Chairman of the Senate Committee on Finance in 1969 made a ten-page statement opening floor debate on HR 13270 the Tax Reform Act of 1969.[17] Senator Long referred to the bill as "368 pages of bewildering complexity." It is now 585 pages and although simplified, it is still a complex measure. Senator Long emphasized the fairness and equity of the bill and believed that there was some justice in the bill.

There were 300 witnesses over a 23 day period of hearings and 7,000 pages were recorded. After hearings the goal was—a fairer and more efficient tax system. The bill included a large number of complex and far-reaching provisions. Senator Long did not agree with some of the provisions. He did feel that the bill focused attention on basic shortcomings in our tax law and did something about them.

Senator Long believed that State and local bond interest was not a proper source of federal income taxes since such a change in tax law would make it more difficult for States and localities to raise sorely needed funds. He also believed that the major objective of the tax reform program is, of course, to permit a fairer sharing of the tax burden.

In his later remarks Senator Long concedes that this bill is not the end-all of tax reform. "It is not the answer to all our tax problems—there undoubtedly will be more to do as we reexamine the tax system over the years ahead. But the bill is the best approach to our tax problems that I have seen in my career as a Senator. It is not only the biggest tax reform bill in our history—it is the best tax bill since the adoption of the income tax in 1913.

Concluding the Senator says, "The test of whether the Senate really wants tax reform is whether it is willing to **take** a consensus bill which can be passed by Congress and be signed by the President. I urge the support of Senators for tax reform in the consideration of this bill."

The illusion that this was a good tax bill was supported by the staffs of the Committee on Ways and Means, the Senate Committee on Finance, and the Joint Committee on Taxation. As you will see later in an analysis of the effects of the bill, it was not a good bill!

**"We Americans suffer primarily not from our weaknesses, but from our illusions ..."** Daniel J. Boorstin.

One of our finest presidents, Ronald Reagan, wanted to do the right thing, and certainly thought he was doing the right thing when he signed the 1986 Tax Reform Act, Public Law 99–514, into law. He considered the Tax Reform Act of 1986 to be the most sweeping overhaul of our tax code in our nation's history. What he didn't know was that his advisers had seriously misled him—they led him to believe that the dream of America's fair share tax plan had become a reality. He was led to believe that this was a tax code designed to take us into a future of technological invention and economic achievement, one that will keep America competitive and growing into the 21st century.

What he didn't know was that the capital gains tax on low income individuals had been increased as much as 640 per cent and even for most modest taxpayers had increased the capital gains tax as much as 150 per cent!

Reagan believed that our tax code became a source of bitterness and discouragement for the average taxpayer. Also that the heavy hand of government has fallen most heavily on the economic life of individuals. The further illusion was that he believed that the 1986 law is the best anti-poverty bill, the best pro-family measure, and the best job-creation program ever to come out of the Congress of the United States.

There were two worse tax reform acts, the Tax Reform Act of 1969 and the Tax Reform Act of 1976. The 1969 act drove investors out of the market, and resulted in high interest rates, high inflation, high unemployment, low national productivity, and reduced growth in our Real Gross National Product. These horrible changes led to continuing Federal Deficits and an uncontainable Federal Debt.

The results of the 1986 law was more of the same as the 1969 and 1976 laws. The United States has never recovered from the ill effects of these three laws. Imagine a Federal Debt of $5 trillion! The interest required to support such a debt is approaching 50 per cent of the total Federal Budget.

## *A Congressman Expresses His Concerns*

In the Congressional Record of October 17, 1986[18] Mr. Barnard was given permission to address the House for 1 minute. His remarks:

"Mr. Speaker, as the 99th Congress draws to an end, I must rise to again express my disappointment that we have been unable to make significant progress toward adapting our laws to today's financial Marketplace. Change is epidemic at both the domestic and international levels. Yet, the Federal laws remain hopelessly out moded. They discourage competition, efficient financial markets, and better service to the average consumer as well as the corporate world ...

"Part of the reason for this and other shortcomings are the financial straight-jackets our ancient laws impose on financial service firms and their consequent inability to diversify into more lines of business ...

"As I survey American finance, I know we are falling behind on front after front due to a love affair with Depression era concepts that long ago should have been jettisoned. We had better get started on modernization. If we do not, then there will not be any American financial organizations at the top of the global structure. They will **all** be Japanese—not just the majority, as is the case today."

That address made nine years ago referred to the restrictions of our regulatory laws upon financial dealings of our broad array of financial institutions. While Mr. Barnard was clear in his understanding of the penalties our financial institutions were paying by not being allowed to compete effectively in world markets, his conclusion that all of the top financial institutions would be Japanese was true not only, from restrictions placed on our financial institutions, but also from the very positive tax policies prevailing in Japan. Policies that clearly motivated the Japanese people to save as much as four times as much as United States people, and motivated their entire economic machine to invest almost twice as much as our economic machine. This high savings and investment has propelled the Japanese economy in the last thirty years to grow at almost twice the rate of growth as the United States. Make no mistake. Their growth has been real, made possible by the Japanese tax policies that motivate people to save and invest at rates nearly two or three times the rates of other free world countries. The Japanese today are the highest contributors to third world countries, and they have amassed the greatest amount of savings of any country in the world.

How is it possible that a country that was totally defeated in World War II, whose factories were destroyed, whose population was demoralized, and whose national spirit was crushed, could rise in only fifty years to become at the least the second most powerful economy in the world? The answer is the powerful incentives upon their people created by their pro-savings and pro-investment tax policies. Imagine a country having half the population and one twenty-fifth the area, and almost no natural resources, approaching in the next year or two the size, economically, as large as the United States. The Japanese have accomplished this outstanding performance not only because their people have the highest literacy rate in the world, but because their leaders have understood the power of convincing their people and their industries to save and invest and to grow and prosper, and to be competitive in world markets. As one student of Japan, George Trumbull Ladd, stated, "The Japanese government and people have shown themselves equal to trying emergencies."

## *How They Change*

ONE OF THE MOST INTELLIGENT AND CAPABLE MEMBERS OF THE SENATE Bill Bradley in Vol 127 No. 106 of the Congressional Record of July 16, 1981[19] proposed a significant change to the Internal revenue Code.

Mr. Bradley proposed an amendment to liberalize the taxation of long term capital gains by increasing the exclusion from the present 60 per cent to 70 per cent, beginning January 1982. The effect of such a change would reduce the top marginal rate on capital gains from 20 per cent under the Senate Finance bill to 15 per cent.

Mr. Bradley stated that his purpose was to spur capital investment, if we are to get our economy going again, we will need a staggering amount of new investment in plant and equipment. This is essential to equip the swollen labor force as a result of the baby boom. If this investment is not forthcoming, we will inevitably see productivity continue to decline and unemployment rise. He states that the change will provide a boost for venture capital, the additional source of our most innovative and productive investments. Also it is high time that we assess the troubled state of our tax policy and make finding solutions an important national priority in the months ahead.

Mr. Bradley also noted the problem of declining productivity and competitiveness. He also referred to the important fact that the U.S. only invests 10 per cent of our Gross National Product, Germany invests 15 per cent, and Japan invests 20 per cent. And further he suggested that, if the World economy is to grow, and if we are going to participate in that growing economy we are going to have to have more investment.

Mr. Bradley said, "If we are serious about providing incentives for savings, let us eliminate all tax on savings. Let us have unlimited tax free contributions to retirement plans.

"This is an amendment which I believe addresses our most critical economic problems—low investment and inadequate research and development—in a way that is consistent with the way Americans have traditionally invested. So I believe that the amendment merits support."

In 1986 when the author was fighting against the 1986 tax law Mr. Bradley followed the Party Line—"A cut in the capital gains tax is a welfare program for the rich"—what economic folly perpetrated on the American people!

## *A Congressman Clearly States that Congress Hides Behind Words*

In page 32996 of the Congressional Record—House—October 17, 1986[20] Mr. Penny spoke:

"Mr. Speaker, earlier this afternoon, the House gave final approval to the reconciliation bill.

"This year the reconciliation bill has been inappropriately named. Nowhere in the bill do we reconcile with the instructions of the budget resolution to cut spending. In fact, as you read the bill it is difficult to find even one example where spending has been reduced.

"Mr. Speaker, it is time that all of us in Congress reconcile ourselves to the fact that we are spending beyond our means.

"We can maybe dodge the bullet this year on budget cuts. But these huge budget deficits are going to shoot down our economy in the years ahead. And our children will be burdened with debt because of our refusal to bite the bullet on budget cuts this year.

"I did not vote for the reconciliation bill because it doesn't cut spending and it doesn't cut the deficit. It is called a reconciliation bill, but it doesn't live up to its name."

As David Hume said, "Honor is a great check on mankind, but where a considerable body of men act together, this check is in a great measure removed. And that body of men acts as if it contained not one member who had any regard to public interest and liberty."

Over the years we have seen bills to reduce deficits that really do not reduce deficits. We have seen bills that cut spending that do not cut spending. We have seen bills that simplify tax laws that do not simplify tax laws. We have seen bills that restrict future deficits that have never restricted future deficits.

What kind of games do the Congress play on the citizenry? Why do they resort to the palliatives—cut spending, cut deficits, simplify tax laws—when in many cases the opposite is true? Mr. Penny made it crystal clear that "reconciliation bill is not a reconciliation bill."

Perhaps Cicero was right when he declared,—**"The arrogance of officialdom should be tempered and controlled."** Perhaps it is not arrogance of the Congress, but it is hoped that it is not ignorance, certainly it is not straight-forward and above board for the Congress to hide behind words like spending cuts, deficit cuts, and reconciliation to defang the public's indignation with the status quo.

As the research into the National Archives indicated there were many people who were unhappy with what was going on in the 1969 time period, when things were relatively benign, compared to the disastrous budget deficits, horrendous Federal Debt, and complex and complicated tax laws that confound even the most astute tax practitioners today.

Public Law 100–119 Passed September 29, 1987 “Balanced Budget and Emergency Deficit Control Act of 1985” provided for maximum deficit amounts of 144 billion, 136 billion, 100 billion, 64 billion, and 28 billion in each of the five years starting October 1, 1987.

Public Law 100–119 may have stated the law of the land, but all actions of the Congress in appropriations and authorizations completely disregarded the law. Were they guilty of a Federal crime? Who was to prosecute members of Congress, if they violated the law of the land? Was Hume right—the body of honorable men acted as if not one member had any regard for the law of the land.

CHAPTER TEN

# The Realities of United States Economic History

## *The Realities of United States Economic History*

While the study of Great Britain's 100-year economic performance was useful to prove the point that high investment ratio drives real economic growth, a more modern study of the United States economic performance since 1950 substantiates the premise that if economic growth is desired, individuals must be motivated to invest in the future of their country. High savings and investment will cause high real economic growth.

In the decade from 1950 to 1960 total economic growth was at a rate of 5.988 per cent per year, while real economic growth was 3.343 per cent per year. From 1960 to 1970 total economic growth was 7.008 per cent per year and real growth was only 3.084 per cent per year, despite the fact that 1970 was a negative growth year after the passage of the tax reform act of 1969. Inflation in the 1950 to 1960 years was relatively low at about 2.6 per cent, but started to rise in the 1960 to 1970 period to about 3.6 per cent.

In the 1970 to 1980 period, total economic growth increased to 10.358 per cent per year and real growth was only 2.768 per cent per year indicating that inflation was about 7.6 per cent per year, more than double the experience of the previous decade. The effects of the bad tax policy were being felt in all economic performance areas. Real growth was down and total growth was up, a terrible inflationary pressure was being felt at all levels of the economy.

From 1980 to 1990 total growth was at 7.432 per cent per year, and real growth was only 2.634 per cent per year. Inflation was at about 4.8 per cent in that decade. The latest data in the 1990 to 1993 period indicate that growth was at 4.768 per cent per year, but real growth fell to only 1.599 per cent per year, however, inflation held at about 3.1 per cent per year for those three years.

The investment ratio, the ratio of total investment divided by Gross Domestic Product in the 1950 to 1960 decade was about 18 per cent, and in the subsequent decade investment fell so that the investment ratio was only 16.4 per cent. For the years 1960, 1970, 1980, 1990 and 1993 the investment ration was 14.755, 14.95, 15.7, 14.58, and 13.98, respectively, showing a trend of much lower investment in recent years.

Recent budget exercises have attempted to hold tax revenues at about 19.4 per cent of Gross Domestic Product. If we reflect on the data shown above, we can see that if your country needs revenues, more investment is required to produce higher real economic growth. Using the above information, if our country had invested in the last 25 years at the same rate as in the decade of the 1950's, instead of running a deficit of over $234 billion in 1994, even with the uncontrolled spending of those 25 years, the country would have shown a surplus of $183 billion.

If over the years the investment climate had been improved so that individuals would increase their investments, and if that raised the investment ratio to as high as that of Germany—about 18 to 19 per cent each year, our country could have been paying off some of this horrendous debt, and we would be experiencing budget surpluses each year to make that possible. While President Clinton's 1994 budget proposed revenues at 19.4 per cent of GDP, in 1993 actual revenues reached 22.3 per cent of GDP.

## *The 1994 Budget Shows They Really Didn't Care*

The President's budget for 1994 actually planned for the following Federal Funds Deficits for the Years 1992 through 1998:

| | |
|---|---|
| 1992 | 386.4 Billions |
| 1993 | 414.2 Billions |
| 1994 | 367.4 Billions |
| 1995 | 358.8 Billions |
| 1996 | 331.1 Billions |
| 1997 | 337.2 Billions |
| 1998 | 374.3 Billions |

Can you imagine that the President really cared about the nation's horrible financial condition, when he proposes deficits totaling 2.569 trillion which could add to the over 5 trillion in debt already on the books? There is no question that the Congress and the President are not working to build integrity and credit-worthiness for the Country. They appeared to be completely detached from the problem of correcting the fiscal errors made over the years.

In his budget proposals the President points out that Federal Receipts as a per cent of Gross Domestic Product are as follows:

| | |
|---|---|
| 1992 | 18.6 |
| 1993 | 18.6 |
| 1994 | 19.2 |
| 1995 | 19.4 |
| 1996 | 19.6 |
| 1997 | 19.6 |
| 1998 | 19.4 |

Even during the World War II years the total Federal Receipts never exceeded 21.7 per cent of GDP and after the war by 1950 Federal receipts fell to a low of 14.8 per cent of GDP. What the Congress and the President don't seen to understand is that the savings and investment climate in the United States is the worst of all free nations. If the investment climate were to be improved so that more individuals would be motivated to take the risk of making an investment, more jobs would be created, productivity would improve, real economic growth would rise, and the result would be a much faster growing economy with improving international trade balances. In the period from 1960 to 1969 real economic growth reached 4.335 per cent of GDP. Since 1969 real economic growth has slowed to between 1.6 and 2.4 per cent per year.

If the investment climate had been as good subsequent to 1969 as it had been prior to 1969, and the country had experienced real economic growth of 4.335 per cent over the last 26 years, by 1994 the United States would have had a surplus of $850 billion! What our country needs is an improved investment climate—a climate that would motivate individuals to save and eventually take a risk to create new technology, new products, new jobs, and improve national productivity.

Certainly the President's 1994 budget proposals are not taxing beyond any level not already experienced, but it is not the level of taxation that is important, it is the way taxes are levied that is important. Savings and investment should not be taxed and there are ways to change the tax laws to correct some of the adverse provisions of the law which impede savings and investment. As the Gestapo agent said, "We have ways!"

# Conclusion

Our brief study of economic history has shown the significant impact of investment upon the real economic growth of any nation. The effects of a nation's tax policy upon the savings and investment activities of its citizens are real and powerful. A nation's citizens must be motivated by proper tax policy to save and invest at a rate that will drive the nation's economic engine to provide real economic growth at a rate appreciably greater than the nation's population growth. Then and only then, will the nation's citizens experience a continually improving standard of living.

In the past the extensive natural resources of the United States have provided a significant economic advantage over other worldwide competitors. As those resources are consumed, that advantage is slowly disappearing, and the United States must now compete on a much more level playing field.

Japan, a totally defeated nation some fifty years ago, has, with almost no natural resources, been able to create national policies that motivate their citizens to save at a rate four times greater than United States citizens. Those same policies also drive their industry to invest at a rate more than double that of United States industry. The result has been a surge in Japan's economic growth over the fifty years such that, in spite of a population one-half that of the United States, and a land area of one-twenty-fifth that of the United States, in May of 1995 Japan's Gross Domestic Product reached within a few per cent of the Gross Domestic Product of the United States.

Germany, also totally defeated some fifty years ago, has provided national policies that motivate their citizens to save at a rate over twice as high as United States citizens, and their industry has been investing at a rate more than fifty per cent higher than United States industry. A combination of tax and fiscal policies have been responsible for motivating citizens of Germany and Japan to save and invest in the futures of their countries.

The acts of saving and investing are difficult for most people, especially under tax policies which penalize saving and investing. Tax policies of the United States must be changed to motivate citizens to save and invest. There are several simple changes that could be made to insure that the saving and investment rates would improve.

Proposal Number 1:

> $1,000 of dividends received by individual taxpayers are excluded from gross income.

Proposal Number 2:

> $1,000 of interest income received by individual taxpayers are excluded from gross income.

It is essential that the total national capital stock be increased appreciably to ensure that the nation will grow in terms of Real Economic Growth, but not inflationary growth. Increased savings and investment will help the growth of the total capital stock, however, it is necessary to provide a further incentive to taxpayers to stay invested, and one provision that would cause individuals to stay invested is the creation of an Individual Investment Account. An Individual Investment Account would be similar to the well-known Individual Retirement Account, but would not be for purposes of retirement, but for continued investment.

Proposal Number 3:

> Each taxpayer may create his own Individual Investment Account. Taxpayer's assets could be contributed to the Account and the assets would have the same basis in the Account as in

the hands of the taxpayer. All dividends, interest, and capital gains would be kept in the Account and be re-invested with no tax consequences. When any funds are removed from the account, such funds would be included in the taxpayer's gross income in the year of removal of the funds. Funds removed after exhaustion of all dividend, interest, and capital gains would be removed with no tax consequences, since the remaining assets are capital which was originally contributed to the Account.

Proposal Number 3 would provide powerful incentives to taxpayers not only to make a first investment, but to stay invested over a period of many years, since the compound growth of the capital in the Account would add considerably to the nation's total capital stock. As we have seen, capital investment is essential to improving productivity, to providing new jobs for a growing work force, to permitting research to create new products, and to feeding the engine of economic growth which is so sorely needed to provide the revenues necessary to finance the operations of the government.

The complications and complexity of our current Internal Revenue Code with its 14,000 pages of laws and regulations, and over 250,000 pages of court cases and decisions, have made such a Code totally incomprehensible to the nation's taxpayers. The most troubling effect of the Code is the uncertainty caused to possible investors, and uncertainty is a terrible deterrent to investment in any form. That deterrent has caused taxpayers to shun investing and saving so that the nation suffers.

Proposal Number 4:

> The current Internal Revenue Code should be repealed in its entirety, as it applies to individual taxpayers. In its place, a new simplified "Flat Tax" should be enacted. All individual taxpayers would be allowed a living allowance and an allowance for each child/dependent. There would be no other complications in the Code. Income would include dividends, interest, wages, salaries, fees, and rents.

Proposal Number 5:

> Long term capital gains should be allowed to be rolled over, so long as the total proceeds of any sale are reinvested within

the year of sale. Such a provision would preserve the nation's capital stock, and permit the most effective use of capital, since there would be no "Lock-in effect," and capital could be free to move into the most advantageous investment at any time.

These five proposals should simplify the Internal Revenue Code as it applies to individuals. But more importantly, they should add to and improve the effectiveness of the nation's total capital stock, which is essential to increase the nation's real economic growth and in turn to increase the Federal revenues so sorely needed to balance the Federal budget, and eventually to reduce our $5 trillion Federal Debt.

There is no doubt that the United States is a nation in trouble. There is no doubt that many didn't care. Let us hope that with the studies made and the analyses completed, some light has been shed on the nation's problems, and the solutions to some of the problems. Knowledge is power—it is further hoped that the lessons of history no longer go unheeded, but rather add to our knowledge of the affairs of men and nations. We can and must see that action is taken to use our new-found knowledge.

Let us not return to the days **"when the busy workers of our cities were turned into idle and hungry louts, and our once patriotic farmers into rebels and lawbreakers, there would arise hosts of men and women, numerous enough, who knew that 'they could no longer live in a world where such things can be'—"** —Josephson's Robber Barons.

Let us arise to help our nation in trouble and prove that many do care!

# Bibliography

1. Ms. Mai Nguyen Woo, “A Time-Series Analysis of the ‘Lock-in’ Effect of Capital Gains Taxation in the United States,” 1981.
2. Hans Tietmeyer Head of Germany’s Central Bank in remarks to Nathaniel C. Nash, *New York Times*, May 7, 1995.
3. Office of Tax Analysis Report to Congress, “Capital Gains Tax Reductions of 1978,” September 1985.
4. “Capital Gains Taxation, Growth, and Fairness” Joseph J. Minarik, Contemporary Policy Issues, Vol X, July 1992.
5. “Maybe, Just Maybe, American Workers Can Stage a Comeback” James Risen, *Los Angeles Times*, August 6, 1995.
6. “The Sources of Growth Slowdown,” Brian Motley, FRBSF, Weekly letter, February 5, 1993.
7. “Competitiveness in the United States, a Brief Review of Research and Investigations” Deborah S. Cohen, September 1986.
8. “Let’s Sharpen America’s Competitive Edge—By Cutting the Capital Gains Tax” Senator Robert W. Kasten in CFO Magazine, May 1989.

9. "Everyone Wants Economy—Without Me!" Walter H. Judd, *Reader's Digest*, February 1976.
10. Christopher Cox Testimony House Ways and Means Committee, June 7, 1995.
11. "The Capital Formation Act," Orrin Hatch Republican Senator and Joseph Lieberman Democratic Representative, *Los Angeles Times*, August 22, 1995.
12. "Capital Gains Taxes—A $1.5 Trillion Opportunity," Senator Connie Mack, *Wall Street Journal*, Summer 1995.
13. "Legislative Update," Merrill Lynch, May 1995.
14. "About Ways and Means," Loeb Rhoades Fortnightly Review, July 25, 1969.
15. Notes From Conference on Economic Policy, September 1, 2, 1995, Jackson, Wyoming.
16. Congressional Record, August 6, 1969, Wilbur Mills opens debate on HR 13270. The Tax Reform Act of 1969.
17. Congressional Record, November 24, 1969, Senator Russell B. Long opens floor debate on HR 13270.
18. Congressional Record, October 17, 1986, Congressman Barnard Expresses his Concerns.
19. Congressional Record, July 16, 1981, Senator Bill Bradley Proposes Significant Changes to the Internal Revenue Code.
20. Congressional Record, October 17, 1986, Congressman Penny Speaks on the Reconciliation Bill.

# About the Author

William Francis Ballhaus was born in San Francisco, California August 15, 1918 and is a fourth generation Californian whose family arrived in San Francisco on October 18, 1846 three years before the famous "Gold Rush" of 1849. He attended Grammar School and High School in San Francisco. After graduation he worked for a subsidiary of General Motors Corporation before matriculating at Stanford University in September 1936.

At Stanford he studied engineering and received his Bachelor of Arts Degree in General Engineering in 1940. He was accepted for candidacy for the Degree of Engineer in September 1940 and went on to his Degree of Engineer in Mechanical Engineering Aeronautics in June 1942.

His first professional experience was as an Aerodynamicist for Douglas Aircraft Company's El Segundo Division where he was associated with the design of Naval Combat Aircraft. Later at Douglas he created two outstanding aircraft designs—the F4D–1 a carrier-based Navy Interceptor and the A3D–1 the first Jet-powered carrier-based Strategic Bomber, which had a long history of reliability and usefulness in the Fleet.

The author was one of the first recipients of a Douglas Aircraft Fellowship, and earned the Ph.D. in Aerodynamics and Mathematics at the California Institute of Technology in June 1947.

After eight years at Douglas he left to become Chief of Preliminary Design at Convair's Fort Worth Division to create the design of the first Air Force Super-sonic Bomber, in 1950 to 1953.

At the start of 1953 he accepted the position of Chief Engineer at Northrop Aircraft, Inc. where he was responsible for creating the T–38 Air Force Super-sonic Trainer and its companion the F–5 International Fighter. His first tasks were to solve the problems of the F–89 Air Force Interceptor and the Snark Intercontinental Missile. He also engineered the Ground Support System and the Air Vehicle for the Raytheon Hawk Defense Missile System.

In September 1957 he was asked to create a new Division at Northrop—Nortronics and managed it successfully growing from 4,000 to 11,000 employees over a four year period. As a result of the success of the Division, he was promoted to Executive Vice President of Northrop Corporation and elected to the Board of Directors in 1961.

At the start of 1965 he was elected President and a member of the Board of Beckman Instruments, Inc and managed that company until he retired in August of 1983. While at Beckman he carefully reduced the company's Space and Defense businesses, and with the effort saved created a new and fast growing Medical Instruments Division. In the last ten years of his management earnings grew at a rate in excess of 25 per cent each year.

He was troubled by the tax code changes which were made in 1969 that critically changed the investment climate for individuals, and made it much more difficult for corporations to raise needed equity capital to improve productivity, to reduce costs, and to provide for future growth not only for enterprise but for the nation as well. The study of these negative trends led the Author to write this book.

Dr. Ballhaus was elected to the National Academy of Engineering in 1973 and served as a Councilor of the Academy for six years. In 1967 he was elected a Fellow of the American Institute of Aeronautics and Astronautics. He is registered as a Civil and Mechanical Engineer in the State of California.